CONSTANCE:

A Force to Be Reckoned With

By

Donna M. Marshall
Inspired by
my late mother,
Louise Daniel
Hutchinson

I've always loved butterflies. This exquisite creature starts as a colorless caterpillar and transforms into a delicate beauty. The butterfly is a symbol of change and rebirth. On a flight to Washington, D.C., I had the pleasure of sitting next to a beautiful 9-year-old little girl named Ruby Evans. She was sketching the butterfly shown above and I immediately thought about my grandmother, Constance Daniel, who fought for change. As I admired her work, she was kind enough to give me her sketch, and I was smart enough to pay her for her original artwork. My grandmother, who was also an artist, would not have wanted it any other way! ~ Donna M. Marshall

Book Editing and Interior Page Design by:
Dana M. Hutchinson
Cover Design by: Tanisha Pettiford

Library of Congress Control Number: 2022915281
ISBN-13: 979-8-88680-033-3

~DEDICATION~

This book is lovingly dedicated to the memory of
my maternal grandparents Victor Hugo and
Constance Eleanor Hazel Daniel,
and my mother Louise Daniel Hutchinson.
If you hadn't started this incredible story,
I would not have been able to continue it!

~CONTENTS~

ACKNOWLEDGMENTS

To my husband Lawrence – I sincerely thank you for listening to every word and story I shared about my ancestors and for joining me in my excitement as I learned more about my extraordinary family. Throughout this journey you have been my rock and kept me grounded. I love you!

To my Dad "Hutch" – At 94 years young, you're still sharp as a tact and still supportive as ever. I owe you a special thanks for acting as a sounding board, sharing priceless stories, and most importantly for believing in me throughout this process.

To my siblings Ronald (Shellye), David (Lisa), Dana, and Victoria (Troy) – You all allowed me to bounce many thoughts and ideas off of you throughout this wonderful journey that belongs to all of us. I love you!

To my cousins Veronica, Makiel, Patti, Beverly, Rashida and Betty – Thank you for sharing so many memories and unknown facts about our phenomenal matriarch as well as our rich history.

To my sister-n-love Dawn – You always seemed to find the right moment to encourage me. You are truly an exhorter.

To my sister and editor, Dana – Thank you, thank you, thank you! You have truly helped to make this book a reality and I am eternally grateful for your expertise, insight, and wisdom. You are a jewel.

To author and friend Dr. Jill Watts – All it took was you saying, "you should write about your grandmother," that led me on this incredible journey. Thank you!

To my new found friend, Ryan Michaels – Your insight is amazing, and your gift is truly phenomenal. Thank you!

To Matthew Keenan (Cousin Patti's husband) – Thank you for getting the ball rolling when you posted on social media that Grandma Daniel was mentioned in the book *The Black Cabinet,* that eventually led me to its author Jill Watts. You literally set things in motion without even realizing it.

And, last but never least, to my Lord and Savior Jesus Christ, for without Your grace and mercy none of this would be possible.

FOREWORD

It is not every day that you're asked by your sister to not only edit her very first newly written book, but to also write the foreword for it! Long before our mother's passing, she entrusted numerous originals (and some copies) of our maternal grandmother's writings, artwork, and other treasured memorabilia from her life to my sister Donna.

As she started reading these documents and began learning more about Constance Eleanor Hazel Daniel, our late, fearless matriarch, she felt an instant connection to her, which caused her to dig deeper and wanting to know more about her life. Our Mom had also started tracing her family's history and began putting pen to paper to tell her parent's incredible story. Unfortunately, due to her failing health, she was unable to complete the manuscript. However, Donna developed a yearning to complete what Mom had started, but with a twist, that focused on a specific timeframe of our grandmother's life including her role in the oversight of the first Black High School in Ridge, Maryland, Cardinal Gibbons Institute, her involvement with President Roosevelt's Black Cabinet, and her endearing friendship with the late American educator, presidential advisor, and founder of the National Council of Negro Women, Dr. Mary McLeod Bethune.

To say the least, I am humbled and honored to go along for the ride on this intriguing journey about our grandmother. Also, I am beyond proud of my older sister's desire to join an elite group in our family of third- and fourth-generation writers and authors. I know without a shadow of a doubt that our mother and grandmother are smiling from Heaven. Donna, you've done them and our family proud.

Although I was born after Grandma Constance's death, after reading this amazing account about a pivotal time in her life, I walked away feeling as if I had known her all along. So, as you read *Constance: A Force to Be Reckoned With*, buckle your seatbelt and enjoy the ride. I'm sure that when you're done, you will feel as if you had known her too.

~Dana M. Hutchinson

Preface

I know the exact day I decided to write a book about my mother's family. She was in the end-stages of vascular dementia and my sister Dana, and I were cleaning out the basement of our parents' home, or "lower level" as my dad always says, where my mom's office was located. I found several manuscripts about her parents Victor and Constance Daniel and their families, but it appeared that none of them were complete, so I decided that I would try to ease them out of the house without my mom knowing so I could read them. But even in her condition, she knew I was trying to sneak them out of the house and stopped me at the front door. In a matter-of-fact tone, she said, "Donna, what do you have in your hands?" I told her that I found her manuscripts about her family and wanted to read them. In a moment of clarity, she strongly suggested that I make copies and return them to her, and that is exactly what I did!

My mother was encouraged to research her family after watching the acclaimed television miniseries "Roots" by Alex Haley that was based on his 1976 novel *Roots: The Saga of an American Family*. As fate would have it, she actually got to meet and spend time with the famed author during a visit to the Smithsonian's Anacostia Neighborhood Museum (now known as the Anacostia Community Museum), where she worked. Because she had the book in her possession, he autographed the book for her, and it remains on a bookcase in my dad's home to this very day.

From the many stories my mom shared about her parents and great-grandparents, she focused more on her father's side of the family and his home in St. Thomas, Virgin Islands. So, I began reading her writings and even though my grandfather had an interesting life, it was the accomplishments of Grandma Constance and her side of the family that kept me intrigued and enlightened. I was hooked. She was one fearless woman and that character trait resonated with me!

As I continued reading, I knew I had to share my grandmother's story. Every time, and I mean every time I found something astonishing about her, I would share the information with my husband Lawrence. Seeing how it was hard for me to contain my excitement he encouraged me to begin writing about her. I'm not sure if his encouragement was a ploy to keep me from telling him every little thing I found out, but nevertheless, it worked. My father, siblings, cousins, and friends also cheered me on, but it wasn't until a few years later, when Matt, my cousin Patty's husband told me that Grandma Constance was mentioned in the book *The Black Cabinet: The Untold Story of African Americans in Politics During the Age of Roosevelt* by Dr. Jill Watts, that I started to sink my teeth into her life even more. So I contacted Jill, and she didn't waste any time getting back to me. After several intriguing phone calls with her, she also suggested I write a book about my grandmother and graciously shared everything she knew about her and the long personal and professional relationship that she had with renowned educator Dr. Mary McLeod Bethune, but confessed she had difficulties finding more information about her.

Always wanting to write a book, but never acting on it, I decided to jump in with both feet. Since my sister Victoria, her husband Troy, and their daughter Danielle are published book authors, there was nothing stopping me from following suit. In addition, my sister Dana who is a professional editor as well as a published magazine writer, committed to help guide me through the publishing process. My cousin Mikki had also begun researching our family, but unfortunately the information she had gathered was destroyed in a flood. However, she allowed me to pick her brain every chance I could and found her to be a wealth of knowledge.

Her information proved to be invaluable given that all of my maternal aunts and uncles are deceased and my cousins who had been in our grandmother's presence knew very little about her. I was almost six years old when she died, and other than what my mom shared I didn't know much about her personally either. I thought my father would be able to share what he knew, but unfortunately, his relationship with grandma was a rocky one and at 94 years young, his memories of her were rather vague. Outside of my mom's manuscripts, I wasn't sure where I would find additional information, for she had passed away and was the Daniel Family historian. Thankfully, her stories did not die with her, for she had given me a grey, acid-free box several years prior to her death and what I found inside was nothing short of a miracle. It contained carbon copies of my grandmother's articles, poems, letters and even her completed SF-171, the application that was required to apply for Federal employment during that time. Also, I found letters and correspondence to and from my grandfather. This is where I also learned that my great-great-grandfather owned slaves.

However, very little was known about my grandmother and her ancestors beyond the boundaries of their immediate family, a circle of close friends, colleagues, and groups with whom she and my grandfather labored with on critical and collateral issues. Her life was impactful, and her boldness, vision, struggles and contributions were nothing short of remarkable. What I know to be true is this, Constance Eleanor Hazel Daniel effectively led from the rear.

I spent days and nights reading about the work of this magnificent woman and even though I was a child when she died, I have never felt closer to her than now. Knowing what I know now, God only knows why it took me so long to look in the box. However, timing is everything and I have to believe that it just wasn't the right time.

Even if I had, I probably wouldn't have done anything with its contents, and my mom knew that. But for her to have entrusted me with such valuable information, I believe that she knew I would do something with it someday and someday has arrived.

Among those papers I also found evidence that made me question what I was reading, and I am sure with grandma's ancestors being slaves and her husband's family owning slaves, it made for interesting conversations between them. I had to first wrap my mind around the fact that my great-great-grandfather was a slave owner. For obvious reasons I didn't want to accept it, but when I saw the 1841 Census records with my own eyes, I had no choice but to accept it. I immediately thought about the words of a song I used to sing proudly during my teenage years by the late, great Nina Simone, "To Be Young, Gifted, and Black." However, if I heard it played today, it would no longer have the same meaning for me as it once did. I feel that way because my mom raised my siblings and me to be proud Black people and taught us about the ills of slavery, so the title "slave owner" just doesn't align with song's title.

However, I'm proud to be the granddaughter of pioneering educators, whose teaching careers crisscrossed the Nation, and who exposed their children and students to the polemic educational ideologies of Drs. Booker T. Washington and W.E.B. DuBois, or what's known as the Talented Tenth, which refers to the one in ten Black men who became leaders in their communities by gaining a college education to reach their full potential and helped them to better those communities and invoke social change. In Dr. DuBois' book titled the same, he argued that these college educated men should sacrifice their personal interests and use their education to lead and improve the Black community. To the contrary, Dr. Washington believed that vocational education would be more beneficial. However, my grandparents saw value in both.

The more I learned about them, especially my grandmother, the more a historical canvass began to emerge. It presented a landscape that stretched from Minneapolis, Minnesota to Tuskegee, Alabama, and then from Washington, D.C. to Ridge, Maryland in St. Mary's County. Reaching into the past to locate, retrieve, and verify salient facts that were either neglected by others or allowed to languish in obscurity, has been a spiritual and an enriching odyssey. Believing that I've been guided by many unseen and unknown life forces, I know that Constance E. H. Daniel has left it to me to share the intricate details of her life with the world.

CHAPTER 1
AN AWAKENING

From examples set forth by her ancestors, Constance learned early in life from her paternal grandmother Margaret Hazel that she was to be a potent force on the matters of race, and not a pliant tool. She remembered her words too. "… and you're not even 10," her grandmother said. "You'll understand soon enough!" These words were never truer, for young Constance would soon experience racism, sexism, and pure hatred first-hand and would truly understand exactly what her grandmother meant. But God!

Young Constance (bottom, left) with two of her siblings, Frances (bottom, right) and Rosa (top, center).

The more I learned about my grandmother, the more I found myself in awe of her, so much so, I wanted my mother to change my name, just to feel a little bit closer to her. To say I was curious is an understatement. When I realized that we shared the same birth month and many personality traits, I began to see where my passion for helping and caring for others came from.

Grandma Constance was born on August 10th, 1894, in St. Paul, Minnesota. Growing up I always thought she was from the islands. I guess I should have paid closer attention when my mom shared her family's history. However, I soon learned that she occasionally traveled to St. Croix and Haiti, with the intention of recruiting and educating young boys and girls, who weren't afforded a basic education. It was actually my grandfather, Victor Hugo Daniel, who was born in Charlotte Amalie, St. Thomas, Danish West Indies (now the U.S. Virgin Islands) on November 19th, 1884. More to come on how they connected.

My dad always said that grandma was a stern, direct, and no-nonsense woman, who did not like him because she felt he wasn't "good enough" for my mother. Unfortunately, the feeling was mutual, and he didn't care much for her either. To the contrary, he and my grandfather got along well, for he said yes when my dad asked for my mom's hand in marriage. Go figure? Like any mother, I imagine that she just wanted the best for her youngest daughter and believed it was important for her to continue her education, which was non-negotiable in the Daniel household. Having a good education was a staple in life as well as a necessity for Black people, especially in that day and time. The same holds true today. My mother shared with me that grandma always told she and her siblings that the mind was the best organ in the body second to the heart, and that they must nurture and educate it if they were going to make it in this world. She told them, "With the odds against us as Negroes, the one thing others can't take away from us is our mind and our thoughts, and the mind is every bit of a weapon as a gun or a knife." Using today's lingo, Grandma Constance was an "Original Gangster" or an "O.G.," if you will.

She came from a good family and was the youngest of five children born to William Augustus and Rosa Elizabeth Grosvenor Hazel.

My maternal great-grandfather was an architect and stained-glass designer. In 1872 he was an apprentice under renowned painter and stained-glass designer, John LaFarge, (little did anyone know that the paths of their children, John LaFarge, Jr. and my grandmother would eventually cross). In 1887, the Hazel family moved from Boston to St. Paul, Minnesota, where William was offered a managerial position of Forman Ford and Co., a professional glass and glazing company. He made such a good impression that he earned a job as the Minneapolis representative for The Tiffany Glass Co.

Standing up for what she believed came honestly for Constance, for her father, between 1887 and 1891 initiated racial discrimination law suits for refusal of service in places of public accommodation. On May 21st, 1887, the *Minneapolis-St. Paul Western Appeal* reported that he "was refused accommodations at the Clarendon and Astoria hotels, for no other reason than the fact that he was a colored man." In one instance he was jailed for protesting; in another he was awarded $25 by the court for damages, after seeking $2,000!

Before returning to Massachusetts, my Great-Grandmother Rosa had two more children, Francis Putnam (known as Frank) and my grandmother Constance Eleanor. In 1899, the Hazels were among those named in an article, "Minnesota Afro-Americans with 'Push and Energy'," that was published in the September 23rd edition of the *Afro-American Advance* newspaper. My Great-Uncles William H. and Frank both served in the military. William enlisted in the U.S. Navy from 1902 to 1905. He then reenlisted in the U.S. Army in 1907 and was assigned to the Second Squadron of the Tenth Calvary (formerly The Buffalo Soldiers) at the U.S. Military Academy at West Point, where he remained until 1920. In 1905, Frank enlisted in the U.S. Army and like his brother, was also a member of the infamous Buffalo Soldiers. He advanced to the rank of Sergeant and was honorably discharged about 1910.

My grandmother attended the Agassiz School, under the tutelage of educator Maria Louise Baldwin (1856-1922), who earned the title of master-teacher, the only African American in New England to hold such a position. She inspired my grandmother who often waited for her with some of the other children, to get off of the streetcar and rush to carry her bags and books. Out of 500 children, not only was Grandma Constance her only Black student, but there were also no other Black teachers under her.

My grandmother was about seven years old when she first experienced racism, but she never forgot what her Grandma Hazel told her and recalled the event by writing the following one-page story, titled "Neighbors" in 1961 just one year before her own death. That's just how sharp her mind was.

"Neighbors"
by Constance E.H. Daniel

Mrs. Schwartz was Grandmother's neighbor-across-the fence. She kept a spotless house and a neat yard. Grandmother kept a spotless house and a beautiful back lawn, bordered deep with dahlias. On a summer night, the handsome old lady would sit serenely on the 'stoop' overlooking her gardens, hands resting in her white apron, explaining the heavens that bridged Washington Street backyards — sometimes to me, but more often to neighbor Schwartz, who would come over to the fence in her "good" apron, to admire the lawn and dahlias — and listen to Grandmother.

'What she don't know!' Mrs. Schwartz would exclaim later, 'What she don't know!'

They were both good cooks, and nothing pleased me more than to be sent or called to the fence, to 'give this to Mrs. Schwartz' or 'take this to your grandmother,' as the two housewives, with little glows of pride, exchanged covered dishes.

But I never saw Mrs. Schwartz in Grandmother's house, and Grandmother never went in hers. This was something of a mystery since Grandmother and her other 'next-door-neighbor' visited regularly and 'went out together.' That both neighbors were white, or that their being so could make any difference, never occurred to me, until one day, when I was called to the fence for the usual, fragrant offering. Neighbor Schwartz took me into her confidence.

'Your grandma is awful smart,' she confided. 'She knows an awful lot. You should be proud of her. Ain't it a shame for all those brains to be wasted! Why? If it weren't that she's colored, I'd want her for my best friend!'

As she lined a pie plate with a bottom crust, Grandmother tried to explain, 'It's hard to say what she means. I don't think she knows. She's been my neighbor for thirty years and she's always been a good neighbor. I like her very much — over the fence. But all these years she's been trying hard to be like her idea of Americans. The way they should act — toward us—for instance. Her idea is twisted. And she's afraid. What mind she's got, isn't hers?'

'Now, Mrs. Rucker....' (Fluting the crust expertly), 'Mrs. Rucker has a mind of her own. I suppose she thinks the way I do, that who her friends are is her own business.'

'It's a lot easier that way,' she added, reflectively.

Grandma slid the pie into the oven, tucked a napkin around a pan of fresh rolls, and spoke briskly,

'Here child! Hand this over the fence to Mrs. Schwartz and stop trying to understand her - and you're not even ten! You'll understand soon enough!'

My Great-Grandmother, as told by my mom, depended on knowledge from the heavens to guide her steps and those of her children into an uncertain future. However, I often wonder what stories she shared about her journey with Constance? Mom said my grandmother was born with "innate curiosity" and had an "insatiable thirst for learning." When it was time for her to go to college, she considered attending then Spelman Seminary, presently known as Spelman College. However, she felt that her Unitarian upbringing, egalitarian views, and advanced educational training at the Peabody and Agassiz schools, as well as the Cambridge Latin School, made her an unsuitable prospect. She also felt the school was not progressive enough about matters that were important to her. Little did she know that one day her granddaughter, Dr. Beverly Daniel Tatum, would become the college's 9th President. I'm convinced that some things are divinely orchestrated.

While attending Spelman, memories of her mentor Miss Baldwin and the death of her beloved Grandma Margaret only further exacerbated an already distressful situation. In 1909, at age 16, Constance transferred to nearby Atlanta University where she majored in English, studied economics and education, tutored other students, and successfully completed all of her courses in two years! Although she was gifted and intellectually precocious, like many college students she was homesick and wanted to rejoin her family. While she was used to her father's work-related absences, she had never been separated from her dear mother before.

Having met Dr. Booker T. Washington while teaching at Hampton Institute prior to marrying William, Rosa was ecstatic when, in 1909 he invited her husband to join the Tuskegee faculty and of course him accepting the invitation. I am confident that she was well-pleased with his decision! In 1911, just two years later, my grandmother followed suit.

Her home-schooling and academic studies were both unusual and impressive for a young woman of her era. During that time and characteristically, women's curricula offered limited general courses and training in the domestic arts. By the end of the 1911-1912 school year, my grandmother had accomplished her goals. With her teaching certificate in hand, she stepped out confidently into the world to begin her teaching career that began in Wichita, Kansas followed by an assignment in Middleboro, Kentucky. However, in 1914 she returned to Tuskegee as an English instructor. I am sure she had many spirited conversations with Dr. Washington prior to becoming an instructor there, for it was he who encouraged her to get "some experience" before teaching formally. What was the likelihood of father and daughter becoming faculty members simultaneously under Washington's leadership? Having an extremely busy travel schedule, he was away from the Institute often. During one of his trips, he visited the quarters where my grandmother's brother William Hazard Hazel was assigned at the U.S. Military Academy (USMA) at West Point. Unfortunately, when Dr. Washington had arrived, he wasn't there and when he learned that he had missed him, he sent him a note of apology. My great-uncle's letter was found in the collection of Washington's papers at the Library of Congress. It read:

West Point, N.Y.
September 26, 1915

My Dear Doctor Washington,

Terribly disappointed not to have seen you while you were on Post last month. I was away from the barracks when you called and when I returned you had gone for about an hour. I had the honor of seeing you just once and hearing you speak …[A]nd since then I have keenly desired to see you again, the leader who has done so much for our race and through Tuskegee put into practical usefulness, the theories that a lifetime of study and observations and knowledge of the needs of our people have evolved, and which have won for the institute the support and endorsement of the whole country. And for himself the respect and admiration of all men.

I am sir,
Most respectfully yours,

William H. Hazel, Private
U.S.M.A. Detachment of Cavalry

Even with a rigorous schedule, many demands on his time, and major health issues, Dr. Washington took the time to reply to William's letter. He wrote:

October 4, 1915

Private William H. Hazel
USMA Detachment of Cavalry
West Point, NY

My Dear Mr. Hazel:

I very much appreciate your kind letter of September 26, and friendly expressions contained therein.

I am very sorry not to have seen you some days ago when Mrs. Washington and I were at West Point. I shall hope for an opportunity to return again at some time in the near future. It was a great privilege to be there and to see the splendid work being done. I was glad to see so many members of the special detachment of cavalry.

Your father, mother and sister are with us as teachers, and we are very glad to have them. They are rendering good service to the Institution.

With kind regards, I am
Very truly yours,

Booker T. Washington

The special Detachment of Cavalry that my great-uncle was assigned to was a special regiment for Black soldiers at the U.S.M.A. Sadly, Dr. Washington was unable to return to West Point. On November 14th, 1915, this enigmatic man who rose up from slavery to become the paradoxical and celebrated leader of his race had died. Tuskeegee Institute's faculty members and students were simply heart broken. There were numerous poets who wrote tributes that lionized the life and work of this great educator, but there was one who had championed him and his cause since the Institute's founding in 1881, and that was my Great-Grandmother Rosa. She was simply

Constance (right) and her best friend, Ruth Logan on Ruth's wedding day.

devastated after learning of his death. My grandmother's teaching career continued to thrive after the passing of her mentor, however she was thrilled that her best friend Ruth Logan lived on Tuskegee's campus. Her mother Adella was highly educated and helped to establish the National Association of Colored Women's Clubs (NACWC) at the school. But once again, profound sadness struck when Ruth's mother had taken her own life. Rumors spread like wildflowers about how it happened, but then those close to her knew that she suffered a nervous break-down and jumped to her death from a high window. My grandmother consoled and protected her friend and refused to entertain the idle gossip of others.

They were inseparable and knew each other's secrets; they were each other's confidants and joked about being able to read each other's mind. Ruth was first to learn, as if she didn't already know, about her best friend's engagement to the handsome and intelligent Victor Hugo Daniel, who had a deep Caribbean accent and was a Tuskegee graduate as well as the Assistant Commander for Boys. With the exception of her parents and best girlfriend, my grandmother kept her relationship a

Victor and Constance Daniel on their wedding day, June 2nd, 1916.

secret. She was wise beyond her years and kept a low profile when it came to her courtship, for she had to make sure he was the right man for her. Clearly he was and they married on June 2nd, 1916, with Ruth right by her side as the maid of honor.

Among many other talents, my grandmother was an excellent seamstress who cared for nothing ostentatious. With the help of her mother Rosa, she made her own wedding gown, and my grandfather wore his military uniform. He was a devout Catholic since birth, and with much hesitation and reservation, she converted to Catholicism. A Unitarian since her childhood, she was a woman who did not easily conform to religious dogmas and whose disposition and training favored rational inquiry and introspection. Her conversion, I believe, was simply an act of her unconditional love for my grandfather, and that commitment would most definitely be tested, beyond reason, time and time again!

Ruth got married a bit later to New York Physician, E. P. Roberts, who eventually became my grandparents' doctor. My grandmother was elated about their union. However, because of life's choices, they later went in two separate directions, but managed to stay in touch with each other throughout the years.

While at Tuskegee, my grandparents had embraced the late Booker T. Washington's philosophy to be "doers of the word," a phrase he often used and espoused to the faculty and students. In like manner, my grandparents taught and admonished their children to do the same. The phrase derived from James 1:22, "Be ye doers of the word and not hearers only, deceiving your own selves." This passage of scripture was their mantra, and they did not only speak it, but it engulfed their very being.

While living on campus they birthed two children. Their first child, Victor Christopher was born severely premature, and no one thought he would survive. Born weighing only two pounds, things looked grim for their frail baby boy, but God! It was at the hands of the illustrious scientist and inventor Dr. George Washington Carver and many prayers that saved his life. He instructed my grandmother to rub my uncle's limbs with peanut oil to strengthen them and he also built a make-shift incubator out of hot bricks to keep him warm and thankfully, alive. She stated in her papers that it was "touch and go" for a while, and that "she would never give up trying to save her son." Her prayers were most definitely answered and through this ordeal and with undying gratitude, my grandparents asked Dr. Carver to be their son's Godfather and they remained close friends until his death in 1943. Affectionately known as Uncle Vic, although he was sickly most of his life, he lived to be 66 years old.

In the fall of 1919, Great-Grandpa Hazel joined Howard University's faculty in the Department of Manual Arts and Applied Science, where he was appointed to teach architectural history, in addition to painting and sculpture. My grandparents, with their children in tow decided to follow their parents to Washington, D.C., while Grandpa Daniel was waiting for his appointment to the Bordentown Manual Training and Industrial School for Colored Youth in New Jersey. It was known as the "Tuskegee of the North," because it had adopted many of the educational practices first developed at Tuskegee Institute in Alabama. Very much like Grandma Constance's father, he often had to work away from home to support his growing family. However, she stayed behind with her parents to care for young Victor and their daughter Marguerite Rosa.

In 1924, Great-Grandpa Hazel opened a stained-glass studio in Philadelphia, but my great-grandmother did not accompany him. Instead, she traveled to Ridge, Maryland to help my grandparents start the next chapter of their life. He eventually joined them in 1927 until his death on February 13th, 1929. His remains were returned by train to the community of his dreams and pursuits, and he was buried in the Cambridge City Cemetery in Massachusetts.

With diverse personal histories and life experiences, my grandparents shared a detest for social injustices and the harmful consequences, shaped either by ideals, customs, or laws, that had already adversely changed their society and lives. Considered as equals when they married, they entered into a partnership that in turn remedied some of the inequities that ripped at the very fabric of their society. Their relationship was a life-long commitment that never wavered!

As a native of St. Thomas, my grandfather was an urbane, mulatto descendent of slaveowners. However, grandma was a descendent of Rhode Island slaves and North Carolina free Blacks. Their combination truly extends the meaning of opposites attracting! Because of their vast differences it was amazing that she met, fell in love with, and married him to begin with. The odd couple to say the least; however, they were connected by ancestry, equality, and humanity.

Physically attractive and a freethinker, with a countenance that matched her intellect, my grandmother was a counterbalance to my grandfather's austere, conservative, and Catholic upbringing. In their declared career choice and long years of marriage, theirs remained an equal partnership. It was very clear that they were devoted to each other, mentally, physically and spiritually.

Nearly nine years older than she, he was well-read, well-spoken, and well-traveled. He was refined and courtly in his demeanor. Grandma Constance needed a partner who was a bit older and stronger to handle her kind of upbringing, for she knew who she was, what she believed and was never apologetic for it. She, too, was well-read and a charming conversationalist who expected excellence from her students and later, from her children. My mother often spoke of grandma's love for board games, especially those that challenged her knowledge of words and problem-solving skills. Together my grandparents found common ground in causes they each believed in.

Convinced that through direct action, education and new economic chances for Black people, they knew they could be a "potent force." They definitely advocated and worked to bring about changes needed to strengthen the underpinning of their society.

Eleven years after their marriage and being a Danish citizen, my grandfather was not granted his U.S. citizenship until 1927. By then, he and my grandmother already had six children and one year later my mother, who was their seventh child, was born. My grandparents married under the provision of the "Transfer Accord." No application for citizenship with the Department of Immigration and Naturalization was ever found for him. As a result, his marriage application was generated without a citizenship status and simply identified him as "Colored" and a resident of Macon County, Alabama. He did not dispute their findings for he felt it would make life much easier for others to accept his marriage to my grandmother. Not that he cared what others thought, but he knew it would be best for his family. He easily could have passed for white, but he refused!

Grandma Constance's parents William August Hazel and Rosa Eleanor Grosvenor Hazard Hazel.

CHAPTER 2

The Cardinal Gibbons Institute Years and Father John LaFarge

Cardinal Gibbons Institute (CGI) was considered as an "experimental" Catholic national boarding school by the Archdiocese of Baltimore for Black children in Southern Maryland. In the summer of 1924, my grandparents were named as its principal and vice-principal. It literally was a school without walls and sat on about 200 acres of land accompanied by an uninhabitable old farmhouse, and not much else. CGI's promoters and members of the National Catholic Welfare Conference (NCWC) fallaciously boasted that it was to be a "national" institution. Well, that was a lie straight from the pits of hell, with many more to follow!

They promised more than they, or their solicited funds could ever deliver. Before his death in 1921, Catholic prelate James Cardinal Gibbons, for who the school was named donated $8,000 to buy the old Pembroke Farm located on Smith's Creek near the picturesque Potomac River in the poor, rural, and little-known town of Ridge, Maryland in St. Mary's County.

Holding its first Congress at St. Augustine's Church in Washington, D.C., Black Catholics were excited about the possibility of having a "national" school prominently placed in the Nation's Capital but because the District did not have an Archdiocese, they had to make their plea known to the Archbishop of Baltimore. Catholics across the country paid very close attention to what was developing at the meeting given that they would be influenced by such actions. They in turn gave their vote of approval to move forward with building the school.

There were several stories surrounding the name and type of school that would be built in St. Mary's County. According to Father John LaFarge, Jr. in his autobiography *The Manner is Ordinary* (1954), a meeting was held on December 7th, 1916, with members of the Congregation of Saint Francis Xavier (CFX), known as the Xaverian Brothers whose mission was to sponsor schools throughout the United States, including the State of Maryland. Bro. Isadore Kuppel, CFX, served as the religious order's American Provincial and was also the headmaster of Leonard Hall, the first Catholic school for boys located in Leonardtown, Maryland. Also in attendance was Bro. Gerard, CFX who stated that on behalf of the Xaverian Brothers, he and Bro. Isadore agreed to help establish a school "for colored boys" in Ridge, Maryland. However, that assertion could not be verified in the historical documents of the Xaverian Brothers or Cardinal Gibbons. However, when queried about it, Bro. Thomas W. Spaulding, CFX, who served as their (Xavierian Brothers) historian replied, "With a nod or a wave of hand Cardinal Gibbons would approve plans or incorporations, but others would take care of business or legal correspondence." Father LaFarge also recalled that the approved school was originally to be named St. Peter Claver Institute. However, on April 12th, 1918, the name that was printed on the Certificate of Incorporation and filed with the Clerk of the Circuit Court of St. Mary's County, located at the Maryland State Archives, was The Claver Industrial School, Incorporated. In addition, Father LaFarge believed that the school was to be patterned after St. Mary's Industrial School for Boys, an orphanage and boarding school for Caucasian wayward boys in Baltimore.

However, before the proposed educational plan could be implemented, the Xaverian Brothers had to withdraw from the project in 1920, and again in 1921, because Leonard Hall was destroyed by a mysterious fire. Ironically, this important fact was not mentioned in Father LaFarge's autobiography. However, the plans for the Claver Industrial School resurfaced, but had been revised significantly by the newly named Board of Trustees, who were already an incorporated body and who decided to move forward with building it.

By the time Father LaFarge approached the NCWC for assistance in 1918, although still unbuilt, "The Claver Industrial School, Inc." was a legal entity. Known to have made misstatements, produced embellished reports, and magnified his role and significance in the founding of CGI, he often provoked others into action by being critical, as well as usurping the ideas, rights, and authority of others. He was the son of American artist John LaFarge (1835-1910), and his mother was the granddaughter of noted naval commander Oliver Hazard Perry (1785-1819). With the founding of CGI and becoming more involved with Southern Maryland Blacks, perhaps it was only befitting that he would come to know my grandmother and great-grandmother, the former Rosa E.G. Hazard.

My mother shared these stories with me during my teen years, but it wasn't until much later in life that I realized the significance of Grandma Constance and Father LaFarge possibly being distant relatives (I'm sure not distant enough for my grandmother though). Great-Grandma Rosa believed her father James Hazard, a Rhode Island abolitionist to be the illegitimate son of a LaFarge ancestor, Oliver Hazard Perry. Ironically, it was Father LaFarge's father who first mentored my Great-grandfather William A. Hazel in the artistry of stained-glass design, in Boston, Massachusetts. Go figure!

Many Black folks learn about their family ancestry through stories handed down, keeping in oral history tradition. If Father LaFarge was already aware or later learned about the possible ancestral Hazard connection between he and my grandmother at CGI, the knowledge might have stimulated and provoked some engaging and perhaps perplexed conversations between the two of them.

After all, he was someone who always sought parental acceptance and developed grandiose schemes to gain attention and approval of his church. This type of behavior definitely irritated my grandmother, and it surely didn't warrant her respect. As you continue to read on, you will understand why. Instead of becoming a part of the solution, he became part of the problem and a much bigger one at that! Although he was not an administrator, disliked fundraising, and most definitely was not a problem solver; after serving the residents of St. Mary's County for 11 years, he knew the surrounding communities and their needs, better than most.

As spokesman for the corporation that held the title to the property in Ridge, Maryland, Father LaFarge sought the advice and counsel of Southern Marylander Dr. Thomas Wyatt Turner, then a teacher of Biology and Botany at Howard University; Dr. Eugene A. Clark, President of the Myrtilla Miner School for Colored Girls, Washington, D.C.; and the new Director of NCWC's Bureau of Education, Arthur C. Monahan whose appointment was announced on February 2nd, 1921 at the organization's Chicago meeting. A little over a year later, on February 6th, 1922, the Archbishop approved plans for the new school for Southern Maryland Blacks. As stated in its Certificate of Incorporation, CGI's mission read as follows, in part:

"… the said corporation, so formed is for the purpose of providing within the State of Maryland, a boarding and day school for the education of colored youth,

where they may be taught the usual branches of sound English education, and where they may also receive the instruction and practical training in agriculture, industrial and mechanical pursuits and in such other subjects of instruction as may be determined, from time to time by the directors." [Sic]

Also, the Trustees pledged to promote "the material welfare of the Negro race through the instruction in an employment of intelligent methods in everyday work and life." Although Catholics made up the majority of its Board, nowhere in its Certificate of Incorporation did it state or infer that the school to be founded for Black youth was to be a Catholic one.

In the Bylaws, Article 1 stated that the Board of Trustees was to be made up of not more than 36 and not less than 20 persons. Article 2 mandated that with the elected officers of the Board, the Principal of the Institute, acting as a member and as Executive Secretary, shall constitute an Executive Committee.

Four months after CGI's official opening, Francis M. Crowley wrote in the Knights of Columbus' publication *Columbia* in part, "… Mr. Monahan resigned from his position with the NCWC, so as to be able to devote his full time, for a few months, to the arduous task cut out for him as Executive Secretary for the proposed Institute."

Of course, Monahan remained in his position much longer than stipulated by Mr. Crowley. So were the so-called Bylaws that were presented to my grandparents a bunch of poppycock? Of course it was, given the Board had no intention of giving any person of color the power to make administrative decisions. So as the Institute evolved, it appears that this unplanned oversight was the genesis of complex issues regarding the managerial authority that emerged between Monahan and my grandparents. If so, then his failure to return to NCWC's Bureau of Education would have created an untenable situation for whomever the Trustees appointed as

Principal. Did anyone other than my grandparents see the conflict that was brewing?

His 1923 article clearly confirmed his views about Black people, making no distinction between those who were educated and those with little or no formal training or cultural advantages. He lumped them all together and felt that all were incapable of successfully performing even routine tasks. Further, he wrote that during World War I, Southern Negroes did not know how to do something as simple as travel until the U.S. Army taught them how to do so. He believed them to be child-like and lacking innate intelligence, as did Father LaFarge who theorized that only the Catholic church could give Southern Negroes what the poet Langston Hughes called "the dream deferred." Perhaps he continued in his preferred position by nothing more than the mere force of his authoritative personality.

I simply don't believe Monahan really knew what to do with the Institute, since it was his first major assignment with this group. Although he held the rank of Major in the U.S. Army, there was little else known about him. He and my grandparents seemed to have frequent clashes and thought that my grandmother might have been unyielding. However, in a letter written to their friends Dr. Roberts and Ruth Logan from Tuskegee, they shared that Monahan was a profound source of irritation to them both; a difficult person who was judged by his titles and "believed" expertise as a specialist in the field of Negro education. Yet no one who had written about the mean-spirited relationship between CGI and my grandparents independently investigated his temperament or employment history.

He was born March 4th, 1877, in Farmington, Massachusetts from humble beginnings, and his father was a shoemaker by trade. In the 1900 Census, he was listed as "head of family." On June 30th, 1904, he married Mary Ellen Cody and the couple had three sons and one daughter. He was an instructor at the Agricultural College at

Worchester for one year, and from 1901-1910, he was a high school teacher and principal. This could be why others believed him to have been essential to the success of raising the proverbial sphinx from the ashes in Egypt.

Mr. Crowley, whose article (cited earlier) continued his high praise of Monahan. He wrote that he served for 12 years as a "Specialist with the U.S. Bureau of Education" and had "a deep insight into the educational problems of the Negro." He also lifted him up as one acquainted "with the method employed at Hampton and Tuskegee."

However, nothing was ever written about his attitude toward Black people, knowledge of race relations, or his "hands-on" experience as a specialist in Negro education. As the young people say today, "he was suspect." What Crowley and others did not know was that many of A.C. Monahan's "progressive" ideas were taken from educators like Attorney Robert Terrell, Black Cabinet member and husband of activist Dr. Mary Church Terrell, and Thomas Wyatt Turner, Civil Rights activist and biologist who helped found the NAACP and the Federated Colored Catholics organization; and even from my grandfather before he became head of CGI after faithfully serving alongside Dr. Booker T. Washington at Tuskegee.

My grandmother, who kept meticulous records, wrote that in May 1924 when Monahan visited them in Bordentown, New Jersey, he told my grandfather that he "should draw up a course of study according to his own ideas and submit the same to him." With the understanding that my grandfather's plans would be presented to, and discussed by the Board of Trustees, my grandparents accepted their positions as Principal and Assistant Principal of CGI, which was a matter that Monahan and the Board neglected to mention. It appears that my grandmother must have been blanketed in under a provision in Article 5 that gave the Trustees power to hire the Principal and other officers that it decided to employ.

CGI's groundbreaking was held on a cold winter's day in January 1924. By July 1ˢᵗ, with four children under the age of 8, my grandparents arrived in the town of Ridge, an unimaginable corner of Southern Maryland. I can only imagine the excitement they had for the opportunity to independently put (or so they thought) their Tuskegee practicum and combined teaching experiences to the test. At last, the chance was theirs to be a potent force and influence young Black minds. I'm sure they heard Dr. Washington's voice in their heads reminding them "to put down your buckets where you are," and "be ye a doer of the word, and not hearers only." After all, this was what they had prepared themselves for.

With no home to live in and only one multi-purpose building still under construction, my grandparents probably assessed the situation with caution, pulled themselves up by their bootstraps, and together went down the road least traveled. What they did not know was the bitter, pre-history of the illusionary Cardinal Gibbons Institute. For as early as 1922, controversy swirled around the very idea of founding such a school. In his writings, Author Stephen J. Ochs talked about a meeting that was held on the third of November at Holy Redeemer Church, a Black parish in Washington, D.C. In attendance were Black laymen and several white priests working to raise funds and garner enthusiasm for CGI. The church's Pastor, Father Francis Tobin, "took violent exception" to the discussions concerning what role Black Catholics should play in charting their own educational course. Under the pretext of conducting an evening service in the sanctuary, he denounced those meeting in the basement as "enemies of the church." In an effort to disrupt and end their meeting, he turned off the lights on them.

The offended Committee for the Advancement of Colored Catholics protested against Father Tobin's misconduct to the newly installed Archbishop Curley and asked for his removal; however, the

Archbishop took no action. For him to do nothing was directly contrary to statements he made soon after his installment on November 21st, 1921, as the Archbishop of Baltimore. In his usual ringing style, before an assembly of Catholic alumni he asserted the need for a free high school for Catholic boys and girls, so that they might cease to be hewers of wood and drawers of water. Now whom might the Archbishop be speaking of? Without specifically using the word Negro or Colored, many heard the phrase "hewers of wood and drawers of water," so it was very clear as to who he was referring.

Cited in Bro. Thomas Spaulding's publication, *The Premier See* (1989), in February 1922, Archbishop Curley used his bully pulpit to urge Catholic Daughters of America to "help Father LaFarge establish a vocational school for Blacks in St. Mary's County that had been planned under [James Cardinal] Gibbons." If not to be a reform school, then it was imperative that the Institute become a vocational one, for in 1916 Maryland had identified and allotted State funds to find an industrial school in Southern Maryland for Black youth.

On June 6th, 1924, when CGI's Board met in Washington, D.C., they appointed my grandparents Principal and Assistant Principal/Matron, respectively to take effect July 1st. But who were the Daniels and what did the all-White Board of Trustees really know about them? Was their graduation from Tuskegee and contacts with the Institute the only pre-requisite for hiring them? As students and faculty members, their association with the famed school had been a long successful one, yet there was no one-size-fits-all who came under Tuskegee's tutelage. My grandparents did not leave their intellect and life's experiences at an acclaimed college institution, so what did the Board expect? They did not conduct separate or conjoined interviews, so was the decision to hire them based on their paper credentials, Mr. Monahan's perception of them, or their need to quickly fill the posts? Afterall my grandparents were Tuskegee graduates – young, gifted, Black, and Catholics, or at least in name only because as previously stated, Grandma Constance grew up in a Unitarian Church and converted solely to marry my grandfather. The second important decision made on that June day was to add "four prominent colored men and women to its membership." They were Mr. N. T. Velar of Pittsburgh, Professor Thomas Wyatt Turner, Miss Caroline Cook of Baltimore, and Miss Minnie T. Wright of Boston. Probably at the urging of Washington D.C.'s Black Catholics, two additional people of color were also voted in as members of the Board, including Dr. Eugene A. Clark, former assistant Superintendent of Washington Colored Schools, and Miss Nannie Helen Burroughs, Founder-Principal of the National Training School for Black Women and Girls in the Lincoln Heights section of the District. However, Dr. Clark was the only Black Catholic elected to sit on the Board, but all others who held seats were tied to Tuskegee. Attorney Robert H. Terrell, a former Principal of the colored M Street High School, and D.C.'s first Black appointed municipal Judge, had also served on CGI's Board of Trustees since its inception.

Dr. Clark and Mrs. Burroughs were well known in Washington's Black community. Each had a public persona, acknowledged leadership roles and impeccable reputations; however, the roles they were expected to fulfill as Board members were never detailed. It's not known if they wanted to use them as advisors only, for the real power and authority of the CGI Board was its Executive Committee, and none of the "colored" members had been named to it.

While Father LaFarge credited Monahan with developing "progressive ideas" that were presented to the Institute's Board, it was both Dr. Clark and Mr. Turner who discussed similar, if not the same ideas in an earlier meeting held in October 1921. Titled "Suggestions for the Improvement of Educational Conditions

Among Catholic Negroes," the two men submitted a signed seven-page typed document dated January 25th, 1922, to Monahan. Was it their past connection to the fallen "Wizard" of Tuskegee that won them their seats on the Board for the appearance of racial balance and validity among Black Catholics? Or was their appointment a ploy? It was clear that they were essential to Monahan's success, secondly as members of CGI's Board, as he had easy access to their ideas. Thirdly, claiming them as his own, he plagiarized the works of others, and fourth, if he had an "acquaintance" with the methodology of Hampton and Tuskegee Institutes, it was a severely limited one. He might have learned of them when he was with the U.S. Board of Education, but he was certainly no expert on "Black education in the South."

Probably at the direction of Monahan and after my grandparent's appointment to head CGI, the Catholic church quickly sprang into action with its public relations efforts. Without a national support base and with the first of October fast approaching, in order to attain financial aid for the school, every Black media outlet was blanketed with press releases. Black churches, as well as social and benevolent groups were also targeted. Flawed information was disseminated often, therefore potential supporters and donors were left confused about the illusionary Institute's resources, mission, needs, and promises.

In his autobiography, when describing the property where the school was going to be built Father LaFarge said that the "very fine estate of some 70 or 80 acres" was purchased directly opposite of St. Peter Claver's Church and that it "…extended from the high plane of the ridge, down to the salt waterfront of Smith's Creek which empties into the Potomac." But in its widely distributed prospectus, potential donors and benefactors were assured that the exact site was a 200-acre farm, part in timber and partly cultivated. Further they were told that the timber was sufficient to provide lumber to all of the needed buildings. To the contrary, however, no timber ever fell, no land was cultivated, and no home was ever built for my grandparents and their children! Yet, and also in his book, Father LaFarge said that in October 1925, my grandfather was presented a $1,000 check from Archbishop Curley to fix up the house that had been built as his residence. The beloved prelate was simply wrong on many important facts concerning CGI. The run-down, uninhabitable farm house was a six-room, two-story frame structure with a screened-in porch. Eventually, with the help of his male students, my grandfather had to roll up his sleeves and begin patching up the place. With no heat in old Sodality Hall, the male students first moved into the rundown farmhouse in the winter of 1924. Equipped with bunkbeds, every available space became dormitory rooms except for the barns that were reserved for the livestock, and no plans were in place to construct framed buildings. Because at that time many Black schools with framed structures (including Hampton) had experienced costly and mysterious fires. Most people knew that such an idea would be a risky one, and if offered, it would have been rejected.

On Sept. 24th, 1924, published just one month before CGI's scheduled dedication, an unsourced clipping was found in the Josephites' Archives that painted a glowing picture of an already distorted and tortured portrayal of the school. With only one academic building under construction, the newspaper reported that:

"Two of the buildings which will comprise the Institute were purchased already built. The third and main house is under construction and will be furnished in several weeks. One-hundred and fifty students can be accommodated. Many applications for admittance have been received already, but it is too early yet, the officials said, to tell just how many will be enrolled for the opening of the new term."

There was not one bit of truth in the previously mentioned statement. It was truly beyond inaccurate and an all-out lie! Was the committee's statement based on information told to them by A. C. Monahan? I wouldn't be surprised at all. As my mother used to say, "He wouldn't have known Jesus if He showed him his I.D. card." In no way would my grandfather have knowingly risked the lives of my grandmother and their children or put them into such an indefensible situation. He relied on his home training and faith, but even more so, he felt obligated to make CGI successful. This was not, nor would it be, the only instance when "news" about the Institute was distorted, embellished, and just plain fabricated.

The Vatican strongly suggested that the American Catholic church begin to engage Negroes in some meaningful dialogue, and like Peter in the *Bible*, go out, be fishers of men, and cast their nets. And what better place to do that than the town of Ridge? While many of its people were poor and land laid unsown, from its landscape to its rich Catholic and cultural heritage, the community was a study in contrast.

As my grandparent's duties got underway at the beginning of July, Grandma Constance's role as Assistant Principal was to start on September 1st. At the request of A. C. Monahan and at no salary, she worked in his office and with school committees until the school opened in late October. This assignment was considered "unofficial employment." During that time, and with Monahan's office located in Washington, D.C., it created another occurrence where she was separated from my grandfather and their children.

While he claimed to be acquainted with the academic methodologies of Hampton and Tuskegee Institutes, my grandparents, who were Tuskegee graduates were steeped in the philosophy of Booker T. Washington and had applied and tested it abroad. They were the real deal, and there was no guessing about what they believed and how they believed it. With the U.S. Bureau of Education and a team of specialists, Monahan surveyed established county and state funded rural school systems in Wyoming, Colorado, Arizona, Tennessee, and Alabama. Unlike him, my grandparents had practical hands-on teaching and life experiences with marginal schools and their students. When my Great-Grandma Rosa, who was the first Black hired to teach at Hampton Institute's Butler Demonstration School, traveled to Ridge to live with my grandparents, perhaps just her presence there might have caused Monahan some discomfort. Also, might sexism have played a role in the bitterness that seemed most evident between he and my grandmother? It's very likely that he came to his new post with some racial bias and baggage. Being highly educated, proud, and outspoken Black women, surely to him, she and her mother, Rosa, must have seemed an anomaly. More than likely, he was blindsided by their intelligence and just didn't know what to do with these phenomenal women.

With no checks and balances system in place and having no clear-cut lines of authority, no doubt a state of euphoria occurred upon their arrival to CGI. My grandparents were most definitely blindsided from the very beginning of their adventure, or should I say their nightmare in Southern Maryland. However, because they disrupted their family life, uprooted their four young children, and relocated to Ridge, Maryland, they were left with no choice but to tough it out. When they made a commitment, it wasn't taken lightly by either of them. Their word was surely their bond, but unfortunately their dedication would take a toll on both of them in the years to come.

As seen through my grandmother's eyes and without pointing out flagrant inaccuracies in earlier quoted passages, following is what I believe to be a more accurate and sensible account of the school's condition when they arrived. Retrospectively, it was published in the

September-October 1927 issue of *The Colored Harvest*. In part she wrote:

"Indian summer in 1924 was a blaze of splendor lighting the long months ahead, and in the midst of it Gibbons Hall was dedicated. When the guests were gone, and the fine cloud of dust settled once more on the country road, the setting sun shone down on an unfinished building, a principal, a farmer, one assistant, a small group of thoroughly homesick students…and the remains of dinner.

A neighboring farmer sheltered the girls and the family of the principal for the next few weeks. The church hall, amply ventilated with leaks became (among other things), a dormitory for the boys. Tables placed in the center of the hall made a most convenient if unconventional classroom. Two tables on the side of the hall served as a dining room.

As the building approached completion, the principal with the boys began the removal of the scaffolding from about the structure. Then the workman left the building, and the "industrial periods" were spent shoveling plaster and scraping cement from the walls and windows.

Until January [1925], the boys kept their residence in the church hall, and then moved in the farmhouse on the grounds, which was their dormitory for the remainder of the first year."

Believing that no chance to teach should be missed, Grandma Constance wrote: "There were times compound interest was taught with a dishtowel in one hand and a plate in the other, but that only served to add a little piquancy [zest] to an already 'interesting' subject." After sharing her account of the day's events, when the only building (of cement and not timber) at CGI was dedicated, grandma did not end the article with her customary signatory, "cehd." She simply signed-off with *"The Cardinal Notebook."*

If it had not been for the gift of $38,000 from the Knights of Columbus in 1923, the building would have never been near completion. The Supreme Board of the Knights of Columbus voted in Montreal in September 1923 to assess each member five cents, and the total monies raised were donated to build the Institute's first building. The old farmhouse housed the boys and was named Boyle Hall after Bishop Vincent Boyle of Pittsburgh. Remembering the dedication, Father LaFarge described it as a "handsome, one-story, brick and stucco building," and "a gift from the Pittsburgh Catholics." The "dormitory" was actually a one-story cottage-style building, with a small common, multipurpose room and two dormitory rooms. With cramped space and double-decker beds, 38 male students were housed there. The largesse of Bishop Boyle and his flock who contributed $19,000 made it financially possible to build the boys "dormitory." Having once been the practice at Tuskegee and Hampton Institutes, in 1925 it was the sweat equity and labor of my grandfather, his small staff of vocational instructors, volunteers from the Ridge community and older male students who helped to build Boyle Hall.

My grandmother created *The Cardinal Notebook* newsletter as a vehicle to report on the Institute's affairs. Still very much spirited and tough-minded, and a "doer of the word," she closed her article with the following thought: "A work so much needed must eventually find the friends and money needed, not only to keep it open, but also to widen the scope of its influence."

My mother, who heard the same from her mother always reiterated to my siblings and me that, "You will be something in spite of, and not nothing because of." That statement has been passed down to multiple generations in our family. Grandma Constance was committed, unmovable, and often unstoppable. Her promise to the school was certainly unwavering. Still, she was pragmatic.

During the years of its brief existence CGI did attract friends, but barely received enough donations to keep its head above water and its doors open. The school existed from one fundraiser to another, and to another, like many of its poor neighbors and partners who lived a hand-to-mouth existence (and my grandparents and their children lived no differently). Again, in 1927 Grandma Constance wrote, "Money, at this time is nil! There is no budget and the Institute lives from day to day. Duns are still 'piece resistance' of the morning mail. But prayer and hard work, coupled with abundant faith are carrying on." For my grandparents, there was always another sunrise of another tomorrow, "a blaze of splendor, lighting the long months ahead." Yet, and in its second year of operation there was a chance to attract funds for the fledgling school.

In 1925 A. C. Monahan escorted Dr. James H. Dillard, President of the Anna T. Jeanes Fund to the CGI's campus for an inspection visit. My grandmother asked if Dr. Dillard would be interested in observing a community group's closing activity for the Institute's Health Week campaign and Monahan rudely replied, "He's not interested in that sort of thing." This is the same man who Francis Crowley later wrote, "his connections with the officials of the Jeanes Slater and Rosenwald Funds, and the General Election Board enabled him to map out for the Executive Committee a comprehensive program, based on sound experience and tried methods in Negro education." (sic)

Monahan's reply to my grandmother more than infers that he neither had significant contact with the Anna T. Jeanes Fund nor was he familiar with its purpose. If he had such connections, contacts, and knowledge, then he would have known that because of Booker T. Washington's influence, the focus of the "Jeanes Fund" was "industrial and vocational education." The expanded name of the organization was "The Anna T. Jeanes Fund for the Assistance of

Negro Rural Schools in the South." Before Dr. Dillard departed CGI, my grandmother boldly invited him to speak to the students. Knowing what the foundation could mean to the school's success, she had to say something. He accepted her invitation and according to her "Notes," he "confined his entire talk to community improvement [and was] entirely unaware that the Institute was sponsoring such a program." Was this one of many blunders by Monahan in dealing with foundations, because it was crystal clear that he knew very little about his role at CGI, much less what the school stood for.

As written by Vernon E. Jordan, Jr. and Ernest Kaiser in *The Black American Reference Book* (1976), between 1882-1932 The Jeanes Fund had given nearly $2M dollars "to improve black teaching by raising salaries or by helping Black teachers get good training." The Institute could have most definitely benefitted from funds for either of those purposes. Tuskegee was a major beneficiary of the Funds' benevolence.

"There is no budget," Grandma Constance wrote. When she asked Monahan about the Institute's operating funds, he told her that Admiral Benson (the CGI Board's first Vice President) was to be told nothing about the lack of funds, as he was under the impression that there was a surplus of several thousand dollars left from building expenses when operations began. Was this a case of the right hand not knowing what the left hand was doing? I would dare to think so! I'm pretty sure it was Admiral Benson who was responsible for fundraising among White Catholics. And there seemed to have been serious bookkeeping irregularities concerning the manner in which fundraising monies were reported and dispersed. Unless and until school expenditures were authorized for approval by either Williams or Monahan, none of those funds were ever handled by my grandparents.

Therefore, my grandmother found it necessary to keep an account of everything that was going on at the Institute from the beginning. *The Cardinal Notebook* proved to be a valuable source of information for those with selective memories as well as myself. The same year she started the newsletter, Monahan, with Admiral Benson accompanied banker and philanthropist George Foster Peabody to the Institute's campus. This is the same man the *Peabody Awards* is named after. Having retired from business in 1906, CGI was much more than a curiosity to the former banker. Since his retirement he had devoted his philanthropy to public service. Peabody was a trustee of several Negro schools, including Tuskegee and Hampton, and the co-founder of the Anna T. Jeanes Foundation. Admiral Benson was thought to be critical of attracting funds to the Institute once it was inaugurated. Clearly the cart was put before the horse since it was believed that Monahan had significant contacts with philanthropic groups and foundation heads. The more I sought the truth before writing this book, the more I saw that my grandparents were being set up to fail, but why? But God!

During Mr. Peabody's visit he inspected the school's physical plant and observed the water pipes' poor condition. Before the school opened, they had been installed incorrectly at the direction of Monahan. Although my grandfather "protested" and suggested that professional contractors be called in, his suggestion was vetoed. My grandmother documented that when the water pipes burst, the entire line had to be drained and large areas had to be dug up to find the source of the leaks in order to repair them. She also shared how it was my grandfather who installed the required check valves. "The principal spent his time repairing burst pipes, thawing frozen pipes, and hauling water," she said. However, when Mr. Peabody asked if there was trouble with the pipes freezing, Monahan lied and said, "Oh no. It doesn't freeze over three inches down here." Grandma Constance was furious knowing her husband had made numerous repairs to the pipes in intense cold weather and snow. Imprudent or not, she corrected the misstatement and assured the benefactor that, "Yes, both the ground and pipes froze," but only "while Monahan was in Washington." This must have been one of many clashes between the "authoritative" A. C. Monahan and the "difficult" Constance Daniel.

And the very next year in a letter to Father LaFarge, Treasurer Williams wrote, "The King [Monahan] can't do no wrong." Fast forward to the year 2020, like the followers of a certain former U.S. president, Williams must have drunk the "Kool-Aid," and probably by the gallons, to have written such nonsense and lies.

As previously stated, when my grandparents arrived at Ridge, Maryland, the only building that was half-way under construction was Gibbons Hall. In his article that was published in the 1928 edition of *The Columbia*, Francis Crowley wrote the following about Monahan's involvement with nearly every phase of CGI's construction work:

"The program he outlined has been vigorously adhered to in the development of the Institute and has been largely responsible for the high standing it has in the educational world today. His wide range of experience as supervisor of reconstruction work in the U.S. Army during World War I, with the rank of Major, made it possible for him not only to care for the purely educational phases of the Institutes' program, but also to supervise the construction of the new buildings, direct the purchase of supplies and envision, as only an experienced executive could, the physical plant of the Institute that was to be…"[Emphasis added]

And given the tone and content about other published writings about the Institute before and after its opening, it's safe to say that it was Monahan who provided the information in the prelate's article. However, the summary of his credentials provided to the NCWC showed neither academic studies nor previous hands-on experience with building construction. Between 1918-1920, as supervisor of reconstruction work at Walter Reed Army Hospital in Washington, D.C., he had charge of the educational services for the rehabilitation of disabled soldiers. If the previous assertion about him is true, then he would have had first-hand knowledge of any possible surplus associated with the construction of Gibbons Hall. In either letters to Monahan from my grandfather or addressed in person about construction matters, whether it concerned buildings, roadways, or chicken coops, his suggestions fell on deaf ears and were overruled or vetoed by him.

Although my grandparents hit every wall conceivable, time after time they continued to stand. But at what price did they have to pay to keep their commitment and hopes alive for so many Black children who desired an education? As the granddaughter of Constance and Victor Daniel, I want to know why? Why did Monahan, Father LaFarge and others feel the need to circumvent every good thing my grandparents wanted, according to the vision and plans for CGI? Making them seem incompetent was pointless because they were sought after, yet other folks felt the need to interfere, and seemingly were threatened by the fact that these two extremely intelligent, well-spoken, and fearless educators could do the job and make it work. My grandparents' experience and expertise far outweighed that of A. C. Monahan, the proverbial wolf in sheep's clothing.

During the first and subsequent years at the school, it was necessary for my grandfather to travel. He met with CGI committees in localities under the Baltimore Archdiocese and trips were also made as far away as Pittsburgh and Boston. As another form of fundraising, he attended receptions with the hope of winning "converts to the cause." He was reduced to solicit money from those who had the least to give. He would give "little talks" about the academic and farm extension program planned for the Institute.

Even then Monahan directed my grandparents to alternate managing the school and going on the road to solicit funds, however, my grandfather modified his directive. He made the road trips while my grandmother's fundraising efforts were restricted to mailings, in which she enclosed a copy of *The Cardinal Notebook*. Grandma Constance shared that by appealing to donors with information at hand, it would provide opportunities for them to see the work that was being done at the Institute.

Characteristic of Black institutions, my grandmother occasionally made trips to nearby community churches and halls with the school choir to raise money. Her favorite hymns and Negro spirituals were sung. After a brief talk and demonstration lessons by the students, a community person would pass the collection plate to benefit the work at the Institute. Francis Crawley reported, "During its first five years of operation, Negroes from Washington, Baltimore, Pittsburgh and Philadelphia raised the aggregate sum of $27,500 for the Institute."

During my grandfather's absence, Grandma Constance busied herself with administrative matters such as the classification of students and producing the appropriate grade-level and remedial lesson plans. Also, she developed graphs to chart the progress of teachers and pupils. And then there was her growing family. On August 25th, 1925, grandma birthed another daughter, Elizabeth "Betty" Ann Daniel. My grandparent's housekeeper Miss Annie helped to deliver the newest addition and proved to be an asset to the entire family. Without her I don't think they would have survived, especially with my grandfather's fundraising efforts away from home. My grandmother would have lost her mind trying to run CGI alone, especially in the condition it was in upon their arrival, in addition to having babies and being the chief cook and bottle washer. Miss Annie was a plainspoken farm woman who lived with her husband John Henry and their several children. Her devotion to her family's land, St. Peter Claver Church, CGI, and to my grandparents was extraordinary and exemplary.

CHAPTER 3

FACING ADVERSITY HEAD ON

D r. Cecilia Moore, who studied my grandparents extensively while preparing her Doctoral thesis, quoted an unsourced article published in the summer 1998 edition of the *U.S. Catholic Historian* which characterized the Institute's setting and the community it would serve. In part, it read:

"This particular part of the state is famous for these things; the first…is ignorance; the second… is ignorance and the third…is ignorance. The probability is that the Catholics of this country wanted to pick one of the darkest places on the map in order that they might brighten up the corner. One thing that can be said without contradiction — "they made no mistake."

By the 1925-26 school year, CGI's enrollment had increased to 60 students, mostly from St. Mary's, St. Charles, and Prince George's counties in Maryland. A few boarding students came from as far as Pennsylvania and Michigan. The students' ages ranged from 12 to 31 years old with the average age being 16. The varied age range caused housing and socialization challenges and concerns. Over the years some of the students were dismissed for smoking, drinking, unauthorized fraternization, and stealing. No student who applied to the school was turned away or left back as long as they met the basic requirements of having successfully completed the fifth grade.

The "Opportunity Group" began in 1924 and provided remedial classes and peer tutoring for students needing individualized help. An ungraded and intermediary class helped students who needed it to make the transition from the sixth to the seventh grade and begin junior high-level studies. Being aware that students learn in different ways, creative, multi-disciplined approaches were devised, and every part of the school was a non-threatening environment and became a learning laboratory where students overcame their deficiencies. With available hands-on opportunities, students were taught basic math, reading and science.

In 1925 the urgency for a girls dormitory was apparent. In his book *John LaFarge and the Limits of Catholic Interracialism*, Dr. David W. Southern wrote that the students were "bunking" in Gibbons Hall. In an effort to resolve the demand, in late December of that year my grandfather appealed to the Federated Colored Catholics (FCC) who were meeting in Washington, D.C. Not only did he propose that its members and friends support the building of a girls' dormitory, but he also suggested that the building be a memorial to Oblate Sister Mary Bernard, who had recently died. The estimated cost of the much-needed structure was $30,000. He also stated that such a memorial "would not only shelter the girls, but would serve as an inspiration along spiritual lines, because of its association with an exemplary Christian life." The Institute's Board wanted my grandparents to educate as well as attract converts to the Catholic Church. Unfortunately, the dormitory was not built, and more than likely the majority of CGI's students attended school during the day and returned home. It is assumed that the few students who travelled from long distances might have boarded with neighboring farm families, or as Southern suggested in his book, lived-in make-shift housing in Gibbons Hall. Living conditions for the girls who boarded there eventually improved somewhat, however the much-touted image of CGI as a "national" boarding school never came to fruition.

Originally intended to be an assembly hall, being severely overcrowded, a large room on the third floor of Gibbons Hall served as living quarters for about 50 girls of all ages. The space was partitioned off to provide room for the female teachers. It only had one bathroom and three showers. The space housed bunk beds on cold concrete floors and when my grandmother requested for inexpensive pieces of carpet to be placed by each bed, Monahan denied her request and in his "infinite wisdom" replied, "Scientific investigation has proved that concrete [flooring] was just as warm as wood." When the girls and their parents complained about the lack of "amenities" in the makeshift dormitory, my grandmother went into Leonardtown and begged merchants for carpet pieces. The girls learned how to bind the pieces together in sewing class and when they were finished, they placed the carpet beside each bunk bed. Also, the restrooms did not have partitions between the toilets to provide the girls and teachers privacy. So Grandma Constance asked Monahan if she could purchase metal legs so the partitions could be installed between the bathroom stalls. Refusing, he said, "Such partitions are unnecessary and are evidence of prudishness and of a prurient mind." Defiantly, she had a local carpenter to make wooden legs and install the partitions in the girl's bathroom.

There were many adversities and achievements at CGI; however, the school was still publicized in less than honest terms that placed in jeopardy the ebb and flow of its undeveloped work. As the heads of this school in name only, my grandparent's leadership was constantly being challenged and held in check, as successful community outreach and academic programs were obstructed. With no committed funding sources, a revolving executive committee, and Father LaFarge's flawed efforts at social engineering, the Institute's Trustees faltered badly.

In the book, *A Great Cardinal Memorial*, Francis Crowley painted an "oh so nice" picture of Gibbons Hall, CGI's main and only building and compared it to that of George Washington's home at Mount Vernon, with a scenic view of the Potomac River. It's ironic that he compared the two given that it was once a functioning plantation with slaves, yet, on the other hand, the three-story, unfinished concrete building named to honor the late James Cardinal Gibbons had none of the architectural style or amenities of the historic home of America's first president. Used as a dormitory, eating hall, laundry facility, and classrooms, to say that Gibbons Hall was a multi-purpose facility was an understatement; and it was never expanded until about 1932. By then my grandparent's had reached their wall of human limitation.

Although my grandfather wore many hats in addition to being Principal of CGI, nothing brought him greater joy than teaching the children who attended there, including his biological ones. The young man standing on the third step wearing knickers is his eldest son and namesake, Victor Christopher.

Although the tuition was $16.00 a month per student, CGI's actual expenses averaged roughly $40.00 per month. Understanding the importance of education, my grandmother relinquished her annual salary of $1,200 and was paid a mere $1.00 per year. Thinking lodging was going to happen in the very near future, she happily donated it to afford her children and others a "proper" education. Still, it had been reported that the Institute was the place to be for students to get a Negro education – "A National School for Colored Youth." Another lie told … but what else was new!

Sadly, Mr. Crowley's false accountings about CGI may have confused potential donors, as they looked elsewhere to lend their support. In their eyes, the school was doing so well, the need for assistance seemed to be very limited. There was no endowment fund and unfortunately the school never achieved the level of notoriety it was hoping for, although it could have. There were, as my mother said, "too many hands in the pot" and "too many cooks in the kitchen" to ever get anything done. In hindsight, just what was the Archbishop and Father LaFarge afraid of, other than my grandmother?

In addition to his administrative and continuous fundraising duties, at times, my grandfather also had to be the teacher, mechanic, electrician, carpenter, and the plumber. And with the constant stress to make CGI a success and his refusal to falter, sadly he suffered a physical and mental breakdown.

CHAPTER 4

A PLIANT TOOL, NOT!

My grandfather was slowly recovering from sheer exhaustion and during that time my grandmother ran the school with the community's support, even with rumors of the school closing. In the midst of these turbulent times another Daniel child was born on September 3rd, 1926, and was named Robert Alphonse, affectionately known as Bobby.

During the 1926-27 school year attendance dropped. The two eldest Daniel children, Victor and Marguerite were front and center in attendance. In the meantime, the Board clamored for my grandmother's dismissal because of her refusal to be submissive, deferential, or easily influenced. She proposed to increase academic offerings and developed a five-year course of studies for grades 8 through 12. Not an initiative of or supported by the CGI Board, it was a "Daniel" initiative, and it was certainly not what the Board had in mind when it first proposed the "Little Tuskegee" in rural Ridge, Maryland. My grandmother also was suspected of altering Tuskegee Institute's model in an effort to incorporate the "dangerous" teachings and philosophy of Dr. W.E.B. DuBois into CGI's curriculum. If my grandfather refused to reign in his "out-of-control" wife, then A.C. Monahan and the Board's Executive Committee threatened to do, or so they thought. Neither by training nor temperament was my grandmother a pliant tool, and she fearlessly resisted those, who from afar would try to attempt to restrict her or seek to erode and undermine the authority of her husband. With my grandfather being very ill, Grandma Constance boldly protected him. Her core beliefs, duly influenced by Dr. DuBois, had been fashioned by her ancestors and mostly assuredly by her father, and she owned them. As she strongly and boldly declared, she came from "right-minded" and "right-thinking" folks.

The Oblate Sisters were a significant force in the town of Ridge, and they must have been a positive resource for my grandparents. As a religious society of Black women, they too, had been laborers in the vineyard. Their acceptance and cooperation of the new fledgling school were vital. The mere fact that they looked like the people they served, and that my grandparents were Black Catholics, probably fostered a rapport and bond between them, CGI, and the nuns at St. Peter Claver School. As pioneers in the religious and educational communities, they understood better than most, the undaunting challenges and possible

With every fiber of her being, Grandma Constance fiercely protected her husband. The look on her face speaks volumes. She played no games!

rewards of the educational work that was being carried out there. Not only did my grandparents worship at St. Peter Claver Church, their four children were baptized there.

While credited with founding the Institute, Father LaFarge only paid lip service to the idea that Black people might have the intelligence and skills to manage themselves and work out their own salvation. It didn't matter how prepared or intelligent it seemed that the paternalistic clergyman never met a "Negro" that he did not feel superior to. That, after all, was his birth right.

Even though he had relocated to New York, he formed a fundraising committee and vowed to raise $1,000 per year for CGI. Called the "Activities Committee," he managed to include three of CGI's Board members and for three years, they managed to raise funds for the school. A similar effort failed in Philadelphia since the Bishop there considered CGI to be an "outside agency." Because 90 percent of the students were Southern Marylanders, this fact alone probably had a negative impact on fundraising efforts. Unlike Tuskegee and Hampton Institutes, the Institute had no well-known industrialists or philanthropists on its Trustee Board to attract the right attention to it. Unfortunately, my grandparents hadn't developed a national reputation or name recognition. In an article titled, "The Immediate Negro Problem," Father LaFarge revealed a glimpse of his feelings about the role of the Catholic church and the pathology of the Negro. In part he wrote, "…the church alone possessed the key to a spontaneous and natural development of Blacks." And he believed that before you could have a strong secular Black leadership group, first there had to be a strong Black Catholic laity within the one true church. It was very clear that he believed that in order for a Negro to be successful, they must first convert to Catholicism before receiving an education.

Still standing in the wings as Executive Secretary was A.C. Monahan who managed to undermine and revoke the administrative imperatives of my grandparents. Many of the problems they faced and would face down the road had more to do with their fierce independence, style, and race, and less to do with their abilities as managers and educators. And as a so-called "Catholic" school, the

Institute needed more than an "idea," and grandiose public relations propaganda to succeed. Not only was it dishonest, but it was also most definitely counterproductive. The school needed funding and not fairy tales. Had it existed, it would have allowed CGI's educators to devote their full time and attention to educating students!

It's rather hypocritical that Father Lafarge perceived CGI to be Southern Maryland's version of Tuskeegee Institute, given that he probably never met Booker T. Washington or even visited the college, but wanted full credit for everything associated with CGI, including all of the bells and whistles that had been touted about the school. Unfortunately, it could not afford any bells or whistles thanks to its beleaguered Executive Secretary.

Because of their dedication to and love of education, my grandparents wanted to expose their students to a plethora of new ideas, but those were perceived to be dangerous impulses to expose the CGI community to such. Yet, it was Archbishop Curley, who in 1921 "asserted the need for …[a] school for Catholic boys and girls, so that Catholics might cease to be hewers of wood and drawers of water." In other words, the Archbishop wanted CGI to turn out "good little laborers" who could not think or act for themselves. However, when Black folks dared to do so, their actions were imprudent, their voices were strident and imprudent, and according to Josephite Priest, John T. Gillard, "The mentality of the 'New Negro" [was] definitely anti-white."

CHAPTER 5

WEEPING MAY ENDURE FOR A NIGHT...

All elements of the Institute's community seemed to be working well and coming together. Mother Mary Cyprian recalled that on Christmas Eve in 1927, Archbishop Curley and Father LaFarge gave the church-school a gift of $1,000 to purchase a bus. Copies of CGI's newsletter, found many years later when Gibbons Hall was demolished, is evidence of that. With no public relations axe to grind, the writings of CGI's students displayed youthful enthusiasm for diverse topics. One student wrote about a donation of a 24-pound bag of flour that was distributed by the Red Cross to more than 60 Ridge, Maryland families. And with excitement, another wrote about a two-acre garden at the school maintained by Bro. Gaffney at Woodstock College, a Jesuit seminary that existed until 1974. He made a shrine for the Blessed Virgin Mary and turned it sideways so it could be seen from any corner of the garden. My Aunt Marguerite was the 8th-grade's roving reporter who wrote about the nine new students who enrolled at the Institute after the closing of "the colored public school at Ridge," and the "County Health Officer" who immunized the students against diphtheria. Not leaving out any exciting news, she also wrote about the school's garden which really captured her attention. Peas and potatoes were planted by the farmers and students in grades five through eight and

Joseph Bush, a fifth grader wrote about a dentist named Dr. Leo Holton, who visited the school and told the students, "Be true to your teeth, or they will be false to you."

Even in the midst of the noise, clamor, and discord among some who wished to micro-manage the school from afar, the students worked hard, and they learned well. Also, the needs of the community were being met. Still, with all of the positive things going on at CGI, my grandparents were constantly met with petty criticism, pressing administrative matters, concerns about the school's funding and its future. With the recent addition of my Uncle Bobby, the Daniel clan grew to six children and my grandmother's ability to deliver babies began to take a toll on her body. Also, her parents, who were now living with them were having their own health challenges, because of their age. To say that my grandparents had a lot on their plate was an understatement! Not surprising though, the tireless pace of their driving work schedule began to wear down their children too. Marguerite and Dorothea, the two eldest girls, had to help with cooking, cleaning, and babysitting. Their chores in addition to their studies caused them to be exhausted. My grandparent's eldest son Victor helped with farming and maintaining the equipment. Not paying attention to possible warning signs, they stayed the course. Whatever differences that surfaced between them, some of CGI's Trustees, the Secretary of the Board's Executive Committee, and the school's former advisor, Father LaFarge only exacerbated an already tense and stressful situation. In due time my grandparents faced serious health challenges. My grandmother had endured six difficult pregnancies while continuing to work under extreme pressure and stress, and sadly, my grandfather was on the verge of having another mental and physical collapse.

The richest church in America uplifted CGI's achievements and its agents, publicizing glowing accounts of its administrator and their work, but withheld the fact that the school sorely needed financial and moral support. Rather than taking a good look at themselves, Monahan, and a few Executive Committee members increased their attacks on my grandparents. Instead of being truthful, they played the "blame game." His hostile attitude against my grandmother was apparent, long before the Institute opened. The fact that he never took ownership for hiring my grandparents and asking my grandmother to work in his office for months without being compensated implies that he must have felt challenged by her intelligence. When she asked that a "system of bookkeeping be put in place at the Institute," his smart and autocratic reply to her was "that she need not concern herself about the books, and that she had nothing to do with it." He then proceeded to tell her that all accounting of the school funds were going to be handled by the Board's Treasurer Laurence P. Williams, although many found his accounting practices to be suspect.

The ambiguities about CGI's management and Monahan's tendency to misrepresent facts clearly indicate that neither the Board of Trustees, and not its Executive Committee had any clear cut or straight-forward policies in place, either before hiring my grandparents or during their nearly 10-year tenure as Principal and Assistant Principal at the school. Those who thought they were stubborn, especially my grandmother, simply did not know them, or her, nor did they take the time to scrutinize the character of A.C. Monahan.

However, it seemed that over the years, whatever little time my grandparents found to spend together, it didn't impact the expansion of their family. That said, on June 3rd, 1928, another Daniel child was born, and they welcomed their seventh, a baby girl who they named Louise Hazel, which was a combination of my grandfather's sister and my grandmother's maiden name. Not only was it important that their children were given names that were near and dear to them, but it was equally important that the names were linked to family ties. I am particularly fond of this child because she was my mom. I'm proud to say that this tradition has continued from their children to their great-grandchildren.

The year proved to be a fairly decent one for my grandparents and CGI. Student enrollment increased, with a waiting list of applicants. According to my grandfather's Annual Report, the students were showing a greater interest in their work; and industrial subjects such as cooking and sewing, as well as millenary work were added to the school's program. There was still hope that the Institute would become a "national" Catholic center for education. My grandfather recommended improvements to the physical plant, housing for male students, and an expansion plan of academic and industrial programs. Only incidentally did he request re-payment for the use of their car, a vehicle that was constantly used for transporting students and conducting CGI business. While the Board acknowledged its indebtedness to my grandparents; they said that there were no funds available to reimburse them.

As the girls' work progressed, the boys' industrial work was severely limited, so they served as helpers to my grandfather. In addition to their academic studies, they maintained the farm's machinery, the school's heating system, and the family car. They also helped to harvest crops from the Institute's garden as well as performed janitorial work. The Board was most definitely getting free labor and they knew it. With the students doing a great deal of the work at CGI, one would think the Board of Trustees would have done the right thing by allocating adequate funding to reimburse my grandparents, but as my mom often said, "That was too much like right."

My grandfather reported that although the Institute was satisfied with the boys' work, he made it clear that they were "not satisfied with [their] situation." He also shared that if provisions were not made during the upcoming year for formal industrial work to include a building, equipment, and a competent instructor, then they risked losing most of their students. When the school opened, my grandfather requested that the Board establish a "Visiting Committee" of educators to routinely inspect the school's site, evaluate it, and advise him of its progress and needs. With the school's current state of affairs, he implored them again to do something. According to his papers and my grandmother's notes, the Board never even visited the Institute, but relied on Monahan's and Benson's reports to evaluate their work to determine CGI's present and future needs. Usually when either of those gentlemen traveled to Maryland, it was to accompany a notable or potential benefactor.

After my grandfather's report, CGI's Board gave my grandparents a vote of confidence. However, Monahan attempted to instigate matters by seeking their discharge. Maybe his concern was not that they were succeeding, but that they were succeeding too much for his liking. Soon after his attempt to smear my grandparents' name, ugly rumors began to circulate about the Institute. Was he trying to cover up his own inadequacies? Were there discrepancies with the "all too little" budget that my grandparents knew nothing of, but probably and eventually suspected?

Grandma Constance traveled to New York on school business. However, it was alleged that she had been fired and left my grandfather, as well as the Institute. Also, it was rumored that a student, John Curtis (winner of the good conduct award in 1927) was going to kill my grandfather and that all of the students were leaving the school. Believed to be a community resident, a gentleman named

Mr. Cole brought the matter to my grandfather's attention and a copy of that lecherous letter was sent to Father LaFarge in New York.

Presumed to be Black, three Southern Marylanders served on CGI's Board of Trustees: Miss Carrie Smith, Mr. Frank Thomas, and Mr. Gonza Wade. However, none of them served on the decision-making committees. Giving the Board the benefit of the doubt regarding their role, maybe it was to provide community input. As indicated in Dr. Cecilia Moore's thesis all of the members of the Trustee's Executive and Finance Committee were "white Catholic men." If Laurence Williams felt stiffed when addressing critical school issues, then Monahan's management style provided no chance for the local trustees' voices to be heard.

As for my grandparents, they were strangers in a strange land, and together they "put down their buckets and cast their lot" where they found the greatest need for their services. With the countless number of lives they touched, they learned to pull themselves up by their proverbial bootstraps. But what about Father John LaFarge?

The report submitted by my grandfather for seven years made it very clear that the school was developing according to the incorporator's directive. He and my grandmother set and met their targeted goals and objectives, while student enrollment steadily increased. Even without proper housing, facilities, and boarding school amenities, by 1931 there were 105 students on the rolls, a 37% increase since the school's opening. It became quite obvious the students attended because of the school's curriculum and progressive ideas of my grandparents, and surely not for the amenities and the grueling work they had to perform to help make ends meet. The needs in 1931 had not differed from those seven years earlier, with the exception of additional shelter and food for the eager students. Due to the inadequate housing for the girls, the school had to turn perspective applicants away, and if the Board of Trustees had taken their initial task to heart, the needs of the school would have been met. The academic programs were developing, and the community outreach programs were considered a success, but even with the progress made, funding was needed and very much overdue. It wasn't as if my grandparents hadn't already given so much of themselves and I'm not sure how much blood, sweat and tears they had left inside. Unfortunately, the science, physics, and chemistry classes had to be canceled because of the lack of space required for laboratory equipment. And while a gift of 900 acres was given to the Institute, adequate training was needed to make the land productive and economically viable. Crops like corn, sweet potatoes, peaches, tobacco, and alfalfa were just some of the items grown. This extraordinary gift of acreage was in very close proximity to CGI's land and in the direct path of the new road that connected it to the school, Leonardtown, Washington, D.C., and other business centers with commercial markets. There was so much potential for the school, but it was purposely overlooked because of the hidden agendas of others and the mismanagement of funds and more. Ensuring that CGI remained competitive with other institutions, my grandfather told the Board, "We must keep the Institute on par, in every way, with the best institutions in its class, if our boys and girls are to be trained for the type of leadership that will ever count in service to the church, their race, and to the Nation."

Had Father LaFarge, who had the ear of Archbishop Curley, used the bully pulpit to encourage the financing of needed facilities and helped to advance and strengthen the academic program at CGI, perhaps the discord heard from Ridge, Maryland might have been abated. Unfortunately he did not; instead, he relocated to New York City to advance himself as the Catholic expert on race relations, and the President of the Institute's Board in name only. Sadly, Archbishop Curley was not interested in or committed to the school or improving race relations. It was written in *The Premiere See* (cited earlier), that when the prelate was the Bishop of St. Augustine's Parish in D.C., he had "attracted attention by battling a convent inspection bill and a law forbidding sisters to teach Black children." But in the matters concerning CGI, he distanced himself and the Archdiocesan funds from the school. He considered it both an unwelcomed and bothersome intrusion in his diocese. Like Father LaFarge and other Trustee members, the Archbishop had also listened to the untamed voice of A.C. Monahan and believed his reports.

Recalling the wise counsel of her grandmother, that when it came to matters of race she was to be a potent force rather than a pliant tool, Constance Eleanor Hazel Daniel took a formidable stand. On July 4th, 1927, she wrote a severely critical letter to Father LaFarge declaring her own independence. Not only had she felt betrayed by the Catholic church, but also felt personally betrayed by the priest himself whose honesty and integrity she called into question. Her letter stated in part, "I resigned Saturday, and I want in a general way to tell you why." "…My letter of resignation gives no reason. It can't. The reason is that the Hon. Board of Trustees seem to have lost what little reasoning powers it once had and has made certain moves, contrary to its stated policy of non-interference which makes it impossible to carry on my responsibilities in a credible manner. I will not carry them on in any other way. They mean well but getting an idea through their heads by devious and roundabout methods, is just about as easy as painting eyes, ears, and a nose on a granite block and then trying to teach it tricks!"

My grandparents truly believed that Father LaFarge was someone they could trust, but they learned all too soon that was not the case. God's word says that "a double-minded man is unstable in all his ways," and clearly this verse of scripture described him. Grandma Constance shared her waning confidence in her new faith, but when counseled, she was told to return to the (Catholic) church and be patient. She replied, **"If I must choose between being a Catholic or an American Negro, I choose to be an American Negro first!"** Of course, the tension between she and the priest deepened.

Not one to compromise principles, she also protested the micro-management by Monahan and others. One example of the pettiness my grandparents experienced was after my grandfather's recovery from a nervous breakdown. He had written a check for the insurance covering the Institute's vehicle but wasn't allowed to mail it until it had first been inspected by Monahan. Completely and understandably annoyed, my grandmother asserted that both she and my grandfather were offended for being treated like "child-like Negroes." She declared that they didn't need plantation bosses nor overseers to aid them in carrying out the school's administrative and academic work. Such an action was not only personally offensive, but it also violated the spirit of the Trustees' agreement with my grandparents. Three days before writing to Father LaFarge, my grandmother resigned as my grandfather's assistant and threatened to take her children back to Massachusetts. Only then did he intercede and offer to address and fix the differences between my grandparents, Monahan, and some of the Trustee members. Reluctantly, she remained at the school and was compensated $1 per school year as a teacher who believed in and was committed to the "brilliant promise" of CGI. Rather than curse the dark, they lit more candles of hope.

CHAPTER 6

ENOUGH IS ENOUGH!

Still trying to make bricks without straw, my grandparents continued to honor the commitment they had made and believed to be their obligation and duty, to provide educational opportunities for the children of Southern Maryland and their parents. They kept their promise, but it came with great personal sacrifices that in many ways were shared by their growing and very young children. They lived, according to my mother, in a drafty, two-story, six-room, framed farmhouse. Not only was it very old, but it was in poor condition, too. They slept two and three to a bed to keep warm, and often caught the usual childhood diseases passing them back and forth to each other. Uncle Bobby contracted a bad case of Chickenpox that left him cross-eyed and needing surgery which left him visually impaired for the rest of his life. The much-needed surgery to strengthen his eye muscle was delayed, for obvious reasons. The Daniel children often suffered due to the lack of income promised to my grandparents that never seemed to materialize. My grandmother's frugal management of produce from the school's garden kept her children fed. They caught fish and plenty of oysters from the oyster beds at nearby Smith's Creek, and my mom's Godmother, Miss Annie Biscoe was a culinary genius. My grandfather's boiler making skills kept that old stubborn and unyielding furnace in some semblance of working condition, so that the old farmhouse would have heat.

The Oblate Sisters who were just across the road and taught at St. Peter Claver were very helpful to the Daniel family and vice versa. In the spring of 1928, shortly after a school trip to Washington, D.C. in their brand-new school bus, sadly their school burned down. The community was simply devastated; however, everyone stuck together for moral support and gave what comfort they could to one another. When the new school year began in September, the resolve and resiliency of the Nuns and students were severely tested given that they had to move into the Church Hall that was without heat. But the Sisters continued teaching school there until November when Bishop McNamara arrived to confirm the children according to Catholic tradition. Father Thibbets had begun to build a new school, and the Bishop returned days later to lay the cornerstone the following day and blessed the Oblate Sisters' enlarged convent. Also during this time children from St. James Parish were bused to St. Peter Claver Catholic School. With the new school being built, there was excitement in the air, but it was short lived, and sadness quickly came to the Daniel home; my grandmother's father William died in 1929. He was her rock and she adored him. However, he taught her how to stand on her own two feet and to never compromise her core beliefs. Although her mother was still living with them, she feared her health would soon deteriorate due to the lack of heat in the house. Being a pianist, Great-Grandma Rosa filled their home with music and taught Marguerite, Dorothea, and even little Louise how to play. The sound of her playing melodious harmonies had a way of taking their minds off of their living conditions.

Once again my grandmother was pregnant, with her eighth child John Hazard. With the help of Miss Annie and knowing that her mother was there, although somewhat frail, my grandmother forged on. At the Baltimore residence of Archbishop Curley, CGI's General Board of Trustees met on May 30th, 1930. Only 11 members were present. With the exception of my grandfather and Dr. Turner from Hampton Institute, those in attendance either traveled from New York with Father LaFarge, lived in Baltimore, or represented the NCWC in Washington, D.C. The proceedings of the meeting seemed rather routine. Following the opening prayer by Archbishop Curley, "the unanimous consent and approval" of the Principal's report was accepted, but no recommendations for the critical needs of the school were discussed. Yet, and in consideration of adults and students then served by the Institute, Grandpa Victor respectfully asked the Board to seek a larger appropriation from the Maryland State Legislature. Agreeing to partially reimburse the school's teachers who traveled considerable distances from their homes to the school, and who remained there fulltime, my grandfather was instructed to set aside $200 of the school's illusory budget for that purpose. Archbishop Curley tasked Father LaFarge with adding three more people to the Board with the hopes of them helping to solicit funds for the Institute. As a result, Monahan resigned from his position, and a gentleman named L. DeReef Holton, about whom nothing is known, became Acting Executive Secretary in his place.

CGI's Board of Trustees engaged the services of the New York consulting firm, John Price Jones, Inc. to evaluate the effectiveness and the school's future needs, as well as to develop and advise the Board of needed fundraising strategies. The 160-page document titled, *"Fund Raising Survey, Analysis, and Plan for Cardinal Gibbons Institute"* is something of a misnomer. With the analysis of its struggling six-year history and with cogent suggestions for future fundraising strategies, it was not a well-focused or probing inquiry of the school's critical affairs. This report seemed to have fallen far short of its suggested goals. Instead of conducting an independent study of the Institute, when formulating their findings and suggestions, the report strongly suggested that the researchers heavily relied on Father LaFarge, some of the Trustees, and the controversial writings of Josephite Priest John T. Gillard. While the value of the John Price Jones report was doubtful, there was some pertinent information detailed in it.

Unfortunately, there was no information stating that my grandparents were interviewed concerning the development and management of the school's educational and community outreach programs, yet the report concluded that there were fundamental differences between Admiral Benson and my grandfather concerning them. Also, the consulting firm reported that he believed that the industrial and agriculture phases of the teaching plan were of first importance, while my grandfather and many members of the Board felt that no consideration should interfere with the completeness of the academic courses. Seemingly the Board was at an impasse concerning the Institute's curriculum. The Jones Corporation also pointed out that Benson and Monahan had failed to formulate an effective financial plan for the school and its Board of Trustees.

In 1931, Father LaFarge hired George K. Hunton to replace the short-lived Acting Executive Secretary. He had great hope that his latest appointee would ease the tension between my grandparents and the Executive Committee. Also, he desperately needed him to help raise money for the fledgling school. Hunton was an alum of Fordham Law School and joined the New York Bar. He had a strong temper and was known to clash personally with his peers; however, he was completely devoted to his new boss.

He also was uneducated regarding the plight of Black people and admitted that he had never been in the presence of any who were educated. Ignorantly, he believed it would take many years before Negroes could provide adequate leadership on any level. He also had limited knowledge about my grandparents, so it was apparent that friction would most certainly develop between them.

In April 1932, while my grandfather was away on travel for a two-week fundraising trip and Grandma Constance was in route back to the school from Washington, D.C., she learned of yet another fire. This time it was at CGI and the fire department reported that the electric and plant house had been seriously damaged. With the help of the older boys, an electrician, and the shop instructor Mr. Marchand, the fire was brought under control, and they prevented it from spreading to the nearby gas tanks. Unfortunately, it interrupted the school's water supply, and once again adjustments had to be made. With the use of a small portable motor provided by Mr. Smith, one of the school's helpers, water was temporarily restored the morning after. Until the damaged wiring could be replaced, the school went without lights, and they used kerosene lamps as a stop gap measure. Because the school had no fixed budget for emergencies and the estimated damages ranged from $1,600 to $2,000 to complete the repairs, it caused my grandmother great concern. With my grandfather still on the road and not due back for several days, she knew he would want to make recommendations to the Board after first speaking with the insurance company's representative.

Respecting her husband and his position as the head of CGI, she grew weary and frustrated at what became an uphill battle. She knew her heart's desire as it pertained to the students and the school's success. However, with the ever-surmounting issues, the lack of respect, as well as the lack of necessary funding from the Board, she was now beyond concerned. Did Archbishop Curley, the Archdiocese, and the Board really want CGI to flourish? Or was their main issue that two well-educated Black people really knew what they were doing as principal and vice principal, but didn't want them to be credited with the school's success that could've been a blessing to all involved? What really was their true motive for the school?

Upon my grandfather's return and the crisis avoided, grandma then turned her attention to administrative matters. An inspection of CGI's physical plant and academic programs was eminent. Because the school was not yet accredited by the State of Maryland, Father LaFarge informed my grandparents in a letter that on August 26th an Assessment and Evaluation Committee comprised of three persons would be investigating the school's curriculum and accessory matters. It included Mr. Carl Murphy, Editor of the *Baltimore Afro-American* newspaper; G. Smith Wormly, Principal of Randall Junior High School (white) in Washington, D.C; and G. David Houston, Principal of Washington's Armstrong Technical High School (colored), who spent three days conducting its fact-finding mission. That must have been a pivotal event.

Upon completion of their assessment, they noted in an 11-page report to Father LaFarge that my grandfather's illness prevented him from being present, however, in his absence Grandma Constance responded to all of the questions asked of her "in a most satisfactory manner." With clarity and great detail, the report reflected a thorough inspection of the school's physical plant, financial status (showing a dependence on sources other than NCWN and the Baltimore Archdiocese), the school's curriculum, and its influence on the community it served. Also, the committee members held an independent "round table meeting" with representatives from St. Mary's County. At random it "made a trip through many of the districts" served by the school. They made unscheduled visits to various homes and spoke with parents and graduates of CGI, and concluded that, "There can be no more convincing proof of the successful efforts of the institution in taking its teaching to the homes of the students, than these homes." In addition, the committee was especially positive in its praise of the Institute's "energetic health program which reached the community." Their assessment varied with A.C. Monahan's earlier comment to my grandmother that "she had nothing to do with the community [programs] and should confine herself to classroom work."

Mr. Houston, a Harvard University alum was uniquely qualified to head the Assessment and Education Committee. By Archbishop Curley suggesting that the report be submitted directly to Father LaFarge infers that he was the one who appointed him as Chairman of CGI's Executive Committee. For a while and by glowing accounts written by the priest and others, my grandparents and the Institute were succeeding marvelously, and still there were members of the Board of Trustees as well as the Archbishop who knew of the continuing troubles at CGI that went far and beyond the bounds of pettiness.

The report also indicated that the school's administration, as stated by the committee, was "energetic, efficient, and progressive." Signed by the entire team, they also recommended that CGI: 1) maintain a student enrollment of not less than 100; 2) upgrade the farm as a more proficient teaching laboratory and the employment of a trained agriculturist; 3) employ qualified married couples as teachers to reduce turn-overs and restructure and upgrade teachers' salaries; 4) ensure that the Board of Trustees secures a permanent income for the school; 5) … because of the low salaries paid, the assistant principal not be permitted to serve without pay, although she may desire to do so; 6) provide special attention to landscaping and upkeep of the grounds; 7) extend and improve the water system given its inadequacy for the 125 persons on campus; and finally, 8) urge that the strongest representation be made to Maryland's governor, requesting the state to increase its annual appropriation from $3,000 to $10,000 a year. The committee discovered that the

State of Maryland's appropriations of $2,000 annually had begun during the 1927-28 school year and continued at that rate through the 1931-32 school year. However, the amount increased to $3,000 annually thereafter.

At last, and after many years of struggle, misunderstandings, misrepresentations, personal loss and tremendous sacrifices, CGI and my grandparents had finally received a fair and unbiased assessment. Even with the relatively good news reported by the committee, they only had a few days to regroup, renew their energy, and with Father LaFarge's input and understanding, make difficult cost-cutting decisions concerning the need to reduce the number of faculty and salaries. With everything in front of them, my grandmother was pregnant yet again with her ninth child. Thankfully, my grandfather's health was improving and together they prepared for the students' return for the fall season.

After two, and probably costly evaluations during that same school year, measures were taken to help keep CGI's doors open. Ironically the NCWC widely publicized the unveiling of a bronze plaque of James Cardinal Gibbons. The planned ceremony was the work of the Board's Executive Committee. Coinciding with the Institute's Commencement Day, on Sunday, May 23rd, 1933, "the esteemed prelate's plaque was unveiled by Mother Katherine Drexel, Superior General of the Sisters of the Blessed Sacrament for Indians and Colored People." With the help of her sister Louise Morrell, she donated the funds to secure the memorial plaque's purchase and attended the ceremony with Father LaFarge, who delivered the principal's address. Keenly aware of CGI's persisting and urging fiscal matters, my grandfather felt that the ceremony was an awkward moment in the school's history. He also believed that this inappropriate showing of affluence would discourage the giving of donations by the very people whose children needed it the most. The teachers who were retained had agreed to a ten percent reduction in salary, and the student body was significantly diminished.

Father LaFarge's friendship with Mother Katherine Drexel dated back many years. The wealth of the Drexel family and its benevolence to Catholic education for Negroes and other minorities was legendary. The Drexel sisters grew up privileged and inherited a $14M trust fund to be shared between them. In spite of her great wealth and finding no peace in the secular world, Mother Drexel founded the Sisters of the Blessed Sacrament. She died in 1955 and in 1988 Pope John Paul II beatified her and she became Blessed Katherine Drexel. Father LaFarge studied and followed her benevolent work as well as that of other wealthy, philanthropic Philadelphians. In his autobiography he wrote that in 1916, Mother Drexel donated funds to him so she could build "a commodious sacristy in the back of the church with a priest room over it."

It was against this historical backdrop that I believe Father LaFarge, then the "token" head of the CGI Board's Executive Committee, engineered the tribute to James Cardinal Gibbons on that beautiful day in May 1933. Maybe because Mother Drexel held him in such high regard he hoped that by involving she and her sister with funding and unveiling the Gibbons' Memorial plaque that they might donate funds to aid the Institute's financial woes. With trying to serve two masters from his New York office with Hunton, he was conducting a fundraising balancing act. While planning the plaque's unveiling, Father LaFarge was also corresponding with the Governor of Virginia on behalf of Mother Drexel concerning the racial discriminatory building codes of contractors in his state. I am almost certain that she had no idea that barely three months after the Gibbons' plaque was affixed to the façade of Gibbons Hall, the CGI Board's Executive Committee would begin closing the school.

It was on that very Sunday after the unveiling that a picture (*see left*) was taken of my grandparents and their eight children on the porch of Gibbons Hall. Other than the smile on my Uncle Vic's face, the rest of family looked a bit somber. It was certainly not a happy picture, but it seemed to capture the years of struggle to build and maintain the school on their faces. Let us not forget that in the midst of "keeping hope alive" my grandmother delivered four children while at CGI and was to deliver her ninth in the near future. While she looked stern and dignified, my grandfather looked confused, bewildered, perplexed, and not well. The unnecessary toll that the school placed on the Daniel family was apparent and little did they know that hardship and pain would once again come knocking at their door. Again, their hope, faith, temperament, studies and teaching experiences at far away schools in Kansas, Kentucky, and Alabama had brought them to this place that day, and that paradoxical moment in history.

The Daniel Family on the porch of Gibbons Hall. Row 1 (l to r): John Hazard, Constance, Elizabeth Ann, Victor Sr., Louise Hazel, Robert Alphonse. Row 2 (l to r): Constance Dorothea, William Joseph, Victor Christopher, and Marguerite Rosa.

Not being able to take much more of the nonsense, my grandmother probably looked back on that summer day in 1924 when they arrived in Ridge, Maryland and wondered what in the heck did she and my grandfather, along with their family get themselves into. How did they not see the self-serving people who seemed not to care about the real reason for CGI's existence, and willing to discard and abandon what could have been a model high school for Black boys and girls in Southern Maryland?

Was educating these children that much of a threat that the powers that be felt the need to sabotage a good thing? Or were they consciously aware of the fact, and they were, that they not only mismanaged the school and its much-needed funds to keep CGI up and running?

Despite NCWC's glowing news coverage of the unveiling of the plaque, they made no mention of the Institute's Commencement Program. Ironically, their press release only gave half-truths about what my grandparents endured for nearly a decade. Still overreaching, it invoked the memory of the historic landing of English Jesuit, Father Andrew White, who arrived in 1634 to the former British colony of Maryland. It wrapped the Institute in nearly three centuries of history past, a history not in the least connected to it. And it concluded with this thought, *"The land on which the Institute is situated was given by Cardinal Gibbons and the prelate manifested a lively and untiring interest in the institution's work until his death."* Perhaps written by Hunton (or maybe even by Father LaFarge), he did not stop to think that anyone would see through the ruse and recall that the celebrated "Prince of the Church," Cardinal Gibbons when Archbishop of Baltimore, died in 1921. Also, his successor Archbishop Curley had served as head of the Archdiocese for nearly 12 years and certainly had not "manifested a lively and untiring interest" in the Institute. Nothing could be further from the truth.

To the contrary, the late James Cardinal Gibbons supported the idea of founding of The Claver Industrial School, Inc. (CGI's original name). That was before the outbreak of World War I, and it was in 1932 when the Institute was given his name posthumously. To invoke the name of Father Andrew White strongly suggests that it was Father LaFarge who wrote the press release. If he knowingly misled the public about which Archbishop supported the school until his death, what else might he have misled the public and others about? While some might not have believed my grandmother, she always said that Father LaFarge was not known to always tell what she called the "unvarnished" truth.

Just weeks after the plaque's unveiling on June 11th, 1933, my Grandma Constance gave birth to the last Daniel baby, named Sosthenes. Sadly, he was stillborn, and my mother said that her sister Marguerite remembered how their father carried the tiny white coffin across the roadway alone for burial in St. Peter Claver Church's graveyard. Without her parents, my grandmother retreated to her room to mourn the loss of her son alone. Even her stoic upbringing could not sustain or console her. She also refused the comfort of my grandfather who was also grief stricken beyond understanding.

Months passed by and the end of the year was fast approaching. With Christmas being one of the Holiest of Holy Days on the church's liturgical calendar, the month of December was anything but joyous for the entire Daniel family. Unfortunately, it was a time of despair. Although CGI had applied for and met the requirements to receive a matching grant for $6,500 from the General Election Board that could be used to pay off some of its debt, and the State of Maryland's $3,000 appropriation was due to arrive in just a couple weeks, on November 2nd, my grandfather was officially notified that the Institute's doors would close on December 15th and his, my grandmother's, and the teacher's services would no longer be needed. Also, it was mandated that he move his family out of the old farmhouse by the end of the month in the dead of winter. On December 14th, he received a letter from Hunton instructing him to turn over all of the files and keys to CGI, with the exception of the old farmhouse. Unbeknownst to my grandparents, the Board of Trustees had recently hired a woman named Helena M. Graydon as the school's manager of business affairs who would stop by to pick everything up the next day. Not only did her authority supersede that of my grandparents, but she was also authorized to make purchases, audit the school's books, and had begun organizing committees among white Southern Marylanders in St. Mary's County to raise funds for the same school they were just told was closing at the end of the month. To add insult to injury, five days earlier the story had already been published in the December 9th issue of the *Baltimore Afro-American*.

Taking direction from her new boss, Ms. Grayson showed up to the farmhouse armed with a letter from him on December 15th, demanding that my grandfather surrender his keys [to her] as of that date. But armed with a shotgun that was mainly used for protection from wildlife in that area was my grandmother who told her to move on after my grandfather let her know that she was trespassing and to leave immediately, and she did. Talking about kicking a person while he's down! Grandpa Victor was beyond humiliated to a breaking point and my grandmother was no longer going along with the program, for she had long had enough. While they may have felt like the rug had been pulled out from under them, they refused to be ordered out of their home in such bad weather conditions with their seven children.

Being used as a pawn by taking unfair advantage of a very unstable situation, Hunton had no idea that my grandfather had an existing contract that had been prepared and ratified on June 10th, 1924, and it read:

"I am authorized by the Executive Committee to offer you a position as Principal of Cardinal Gibbons Institute, to begin work on July 1, 1924, at a salary of $2,500 per year, **together with a residence with heat, lights and fuel for yourself and family.** *Your necessary traveling expenses will be paid when you are in the field for the Institute. The arrangement is to continue indefinitely with* **the understanding that it may be terminated by**

either the Board of Trustees or by the Principal provided thirty days is given, if at the end of the regular school year, or ninety days if during the school year."

It was apparent that Hunton hadn't done his homework and had violated my grandfather's contract. Since Attorney Terrell had died six years prior, my grandfather had to bring it to his attention. Father LaFarge knew that his appointee was unsuitable for his position, however he hired him anyway and the manner in which he paid him was rather suspect.

As the Trustee's Executive Secretary, he was paid an annual salary of $4,000 that was funded by Mother Katherine Drexel, her sister Ms. Morrell, and the Trustees of CGI. Father LaFarge may have defended Hunton's appointment, but if he thought that my grandmother would remain silent about it, he had another thing coming and was gravely mistaken. She had no problems expressing her feelings and wrote a letter to Father LaFarge questioning his appointee's qualifications, given he was known for not making sound judgements. However, Father LaFarge refused to admit his limitations and shortcomings. As a result, CGI's debts continued to mount, my grandparents were not consulted about them, nor were they included in the ill-conceived plan, however, they pushed back vehemently and openly criticized the latest scheme of illogical management orchestrated by NCWC. Their actions had irreparably harmed the school's welfare and raised questions about its credibility. Reckless with their hasty actions, Hunton and the Executive Committee had made no provisions for closing the school or maintaining its records that were housed next door at St. Peter Claver Church which caught fire on March 13th, 1934, destroying everything. God in His infinite wisdom was trying to tell them something, but they refused to listen because they were too busy plotting evil.

As if they hadn't been through enough, another family matter plagued my grandparents concerning their son Victor Christopher, who had experienced racism first-hand after applying to Catholic University to attend college. How ironic, given that six years earlier, in 1927 my grandmother had already made her position on racism in the Catholic church crystal clear in a letter to Father LaFarge. In her opinion, she stated that if racism was not promoted by the church, then certainly its silence and tolerance of it made them culpable, and its recommendation of prayer and patience as a remedy indefensible. The fact that Black Catholics continued to be segregated in every aspect of their secular and religious lives was arguably an offensive and repugnant one. From birth to the grave, based solely on skin color and ethnicity, and on the presumption of mental and social inferiority, racial tolerance was a daily occurrence in the lives of Black folk. Always adamant about his faith, and possibly to a fault in my opinion, Grandpa Victor harshly and forcefully defended the Catholic Church and opposed those who openly criticized it. Often, he was apologetic for it, and like Job who was tested by satan and loss everything, but still unwavering in his love for God, his belief in Catholicism was the same, but he would soon see that the church he rigorously defended was far from the same God that Job knew because of their actions. One knows a tree by the fruit that it bears!

While some thought his subsequent actions were irrational and even reckless, my grandfather was deeply concerned that his eldest son would possibly be judged unfairly and harmed unjustly by the very church he was extremely devoted to solely because of the color of his skin. Yet, my grandparents still had high hopes, not only for my Uncle Vic, but for the Catholic church too, for it was reported that Black nuns were allowed to take evening courses at Catholic University, hopefully opening a door for their son and other Black people to attend also. But as they would soon find out, it was not an equal opportunity college for all.

Sadly, my grandparents suffered enough at the hands of the church, yet again my grandfather was hurt, this time to learn that the school had denied his son attendance just because he was Black. Although that wasn't directly stated as the reason in the letter they received, my grandparents knew better. So my grandfather immediately wrote a very perfunctory letter to the school's registrar, outlining the continuous sacrifices and support made by them on behalf of the church, but it fell on deaf ears. He eventually received an answer to his letter and in part, it read, "Answering your letter: I am directed to very kindly state that it will be entirely impractical for your son to apply for admission to the University." No matter how "kindly" their denial was worded, the work "kindly" in no way softened the school's offensive response. As a result, Grandpa Daniel could no longer remain ambiguous about the subject of racism in the Catholic Church of America. With him no longer being a citizen of the Danish West Indies or a "nominal" Negro, he was truly treated like an American Negro.

After a long letter writing campaign on his son's behalf, and being extremely disappointed repeatedly, it was suggested by one of the priests that he reach out to Archbishop Curley for help; the one man who clearly showed his disdain for my grandparents and for Negroes period. No such correspondence was found to verify that my grandfather had actually written to the prelate; and I am certainly not surprised. Eventually, young Victor enrolled and was accepted at Hampton Institute. However, my grandparents never anticipated that another and even more crushing blow was coming their way.

Betty Ann, my grandparents first child born at CGI became ill and had to be taken to Children's Hospital in Washington, D.C. Because of the severity of her illness, sadly on January 8th, 1934, she passed away at the age of 8. I remember my mother sharing that she earnestly believed that her life patterned after her mother's. For she too had a child who was stillborn and a son who died at the same hospital, and almost the same age. Because Betty had been diagnosed with rheumatic fever, her weakened heart could not withstand the lack of heat in my grandparent's home. According to my mother, they felt that other factors and mean-spirited circumstances contributed to her death as well. At the end of January, my grandfather wrote to Archbishop Curley. In part he said:

"Your Grace: The temperature in my house is at the present 54 degrees because the Executive Committee persistently refused to live up to its agreement to furnish fuel. Two weeks ago, I buried an eight-year-old child of mine. This child lost her life because I was unable to properly provide for her…"

Riddled with guilt and shouldering the entire responsibility for the death of his daughter, my grandfather was simply devastated! But the guilt was not his to shoulder alone, for when employed by the Institute, he was contractually guaranteed that the CGI Corporation directed by its Board of Directors would provide heat for their home (the furnace required hard coal, not green wood). His letter to the Archbishop stirred no sympathy or compassion, and it went unanswered. Did he have that much hate in his heart that he could not muster any compassion, for not even a child? It was only Sister Philomena, an Oblate Nun, who showed love and compassion for the Daniel family in their time of bereavement. My grandmother, who was hurt, tired, and bitter refused to bring her child back to Ridge for burial and instead, laid Betty Ann to rest in the "Colored" section of Mt. Olivet Cemetery in Washington, D.C.

A decade of living a hand-to-mouth existence, making bricks without straw, endless fundraising, fencing with detractors, all while giving birth to children and burying them too, all while helping to run a school to educate children from near and afar, was all about to come to an end. Creativity, resiliency, and dedicated to tightly held beliefs all exacted their price and had their limits! And the admonishments not to be "a pliant tool" or yield convictions and principles for expediency, personal gain and comfort had exacted a price incapable of rational comprehension. My grandparents withstood many indignities, suffered and sacrificed much, but their greatest agony was the seemingly needless loss of a child. My grandfather closed his letter to the Archbishop with this question: "Is this the best my Catholic friends can do for me?" Not only was he pained by the loss of an innocent child, but he was also bewildered and dismayed by the uncharitable actions taken by agents of the church. Still, the Archbishop kept his distance and remained silent, and the Catholic church stayed dispassionately detached and ever removed by the death of my grandparent's 8-year-old daughter.

The hypocrisy was deafening given how Archbishop Curley routinely sent letters from them to Father LaFarge, and how both clerics who once professed to love Betty Ann as a member of the Body of Christ never acknowledged her death, much less sent any kind of condolences. However, hanging in my parents' home today is a letter of condolence (pictured right) sent to my grandparents from Dr. George Washington Carver, expressing sympathy for her death. It reads:

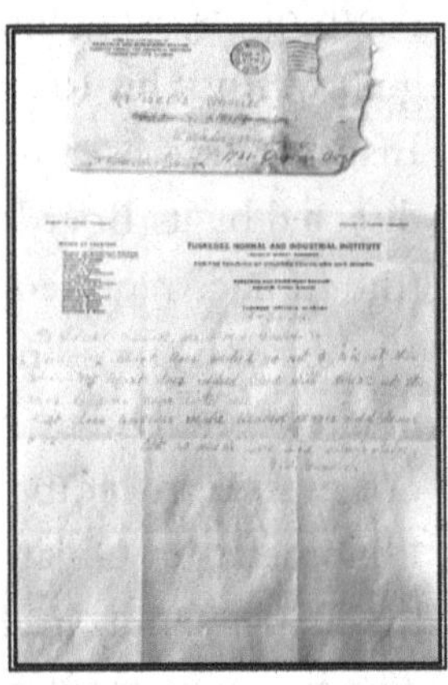

Letter of Condolence from Dr. George Washington Carver to Victor and Constance Daniel after the death of their daughter Betty Ann.

ജ   ജ   ജ

Although the school had closed, my grandfather's contract still had to be honored, allowing he, my grandmother and their children to live in the old farmhouse until April 1ˢᵗ, 1934, the date they moved out. Conducting business in decency and in order, it wasn't until then that my grandfather returned CGI's keys and files to Ms. Graydon at the Law Office of John Biscoe. However, Grandma Constance simply trusted no one at this juncture and needed witnesses to verify that everything had been turned in upon their departure. Shortly thereafter Father LaFarge and Ms. Graydon met with an all-white community group to come up with plans to eventually re-open CGI as a day school. Foolishly they thought it would be easy trying to use the foundation my grandparents had already laid, but it wasn't.

The Dedication of Cardinal Gibbons Institute in 1925. On the first row, fourth from the right is Alum Alice Bennett and on the second row, in the center is Father John LaFarge with Victor and Constance Daniel to the left and right of him.

Years later however, when the old Gibbons Hall was demolished, even more of my grandparent's records were lost as well. Ironically, an old metal cabinet filled with some of their files was untouched by the recking ball. CGI alum Alice Bennett, who is pictured standing next to my Aunt Marguerite in the photograph taken the day of CGI's Dedication, had placed them there for safe keeping. Look at God!

Still owed back-pay, my grandfather insisted that the Trustees honor their commitment to he and his wife, but they denied his claim of monies due. Fearing adverse publicity, knowing that he was prepared to take the Archdiocese to court, Archbishop Curley reluctantly paid him the sum of $1,338.06. Also, he knew that by engaging my grandparents in a court battle would most likely prove my grandfather's claim that the amount owed to him was much more. With Grandma Constance armed with pen, paper, and her sharp intellect, she was prepared to expose everyone. The auditor however reported that my grandfather was due $2,210.06 in salary through the end of the year.

When the school closed, Father LaFarge had abandoned my grandparents, the teachers, and the 140 students who were enrolled. Sadly, it left the teachers jobless and homeless, and the entire community of Ridge in dismay and disarray. The official reason given by the Archdiocese for CGI's closing was an indebtedness of $15,000 and the Great Depression. That most definitely was damage control and of course another lie told.

However, that sent my grandmother over the edge, for enough was enough. How long were they going to try and cover up the mismanagement by the Executive Committee, A.C. Monahan, the Board of Trustees, and others? How long was the Archbishop going to pretend he remotely cared about CGI? How long were they going to deny the fact that the Institute was a success, and it was the powers that be, with their inexperience and prejudices who truly caused the school to close and negating what would have been a blessing to all around? Just, how long?

Grandma Constance was having none of it after hearing the Archbishop's statement that "the Institute was an absolute failure." It was apparent they had no clue who Victor Daniel's wife really was, and in defense of her husband, on April 14, 1934, she wrote a very direct letter to Archbishop Curley. She asserted that the people of St. Mary's County as well as the neighboring counties had the right to know exactly what happened to CGI. She was neither "intractable" nor a "nominal" Catholic as she had been described. As mentioned previously, while she converted to Catholicism, it was solely to be on one accord with my grandfather before marrying him, and her conversion was in name only. The fact that she questioned and challenged overt racism in the Catholic church was entirely characteristic of her, and should have not surprised a soul, however it surprised many. After all, she was the embodiment of her ancestors, and a principled Black woman! Continuing, she wrote: "Suppression of truth-a-la LaFarge, won't do it. Piety veneered hypocrisy won't do it. Patronizing and flattery won't do it." Referring to herself she said, "I have received enough attempted domination to have crippled an average person. However, I am not average because I come from generations of people who knew what was needed for the welfare of their race and budged not one inch for anyone, in the fulfillment of their moral obligations. Most Negroes are better than average. They have to overcome more to get anywhere."

Principled to a fault, she was the same Constance Daniel whose Grandpa Hazel was held in the Cuyahoga County Jail in Ohio for defending the rights of a fugitive slave; the same Constance Daniel whose father fled oppression in North Carolina with she and the rest of his family on foot and with a cart, that took almost three years to arrive in Massachusetts, our Nation's "cradle of liberty." She's the same Constance Daniel whose father also refused to accept second-class citizenship and was denied service in places of public accommodation between the late 1880's and early 1890's in defense of his rights as a Black man. Like Jesus, she was the same from the day she was born until the day she took her last breath!

She also reminded the Archbishop about her daughter's death and how she found her at home struggling to get warm using the green timber for heat instead of the hard coal that had been promised to her husband in his contract. Although my grandfather was quite shaken behind all of this, he was a forgiving man, and he remained a devout Catholic. While he did not blame the church overall, he did hold the people who were in charge accountable. However to the contrary, my grandmother wanted nothing more to do with Catholicism and returned to her Unitarian roots. She never stepped foot into a Catholic church again; nor did she and my grandfather openly speak of the loss of their two children during their tenure at CGI.

Contrary to what others thought and had the audacity to say, the Institute was not a failure, and neither were my grandparents. Despite the efforts of many whites who tried to point their ugly fingers at them, their thumbs were pointing right back at themselves. An atypical school, CGI provided the students as well as the community sound academic studies and culturally rich programs. They learned in a non-threatening environment with a non-threatening approach. Meeting their critical needs daily, like the spokes of a wheel, the Institute's programs radiated out into neighboring and outlying communities. Also, my grandparent's outreach efforts included health, sanitation, hygiene, parenting, home improvement and agricultural programs. In very real terms, none before them had selflessly given or wrought as much good. No one worked harder or more faithfully than they had, yet so many seemed unappreciative. Anything worth fighting for doesn't come easy and always at a cost. My grandparents knew that all too well. The following poem was republished the year they were married and ironically enough, it sums up their journey at Cardinal Gibbons Institute.

"The Road Not Taken"
by Robert Frost (1916)

I shall be telling this
with a sigh
Somewhere ages and ages
hence:
Two roads diverged in a
wood, and I
I took the one less
traveled by,
And this has made all the
difference.

(Reprinted the same year
Constance married Victor.)

The beautiful Constance Daniel on the grounds of Tuskegee Institute.

Grandma Constance standing on the
porch of her home
in the District of Columbia.

Not From the Bible

He that hath done nothing, the same shall now raise Cain; be he that hath diligently tried to do something with nothing, the same shall now raise chickens and hogs in peace, even until the end of his days.

~CEHD

CHAPTER 7

...BUT JOY COMES IN THE MORNING

It was a beautiful spring day when the Daniel family packed up their belongings and returned to Washington, D.C. My mother barely recalled the trip from Ridge, but she did remember the feeling of excitement knowing they were finally leaving that old, cold, cramped farmhouse and how it took several men to get her Grandma Rosa's cherished piano on the back of the truck. They were not going to leave behind the one thing that brought them joy.

However, before returning to the District she made sure she found employment and was hired by *The Afro-American* newspaper. She also secured funding to refinance her uncle's home located at 905 Westminster Street, in Northwest, where she and her family could live comfortably. After their arrival, the five youngest Daniel children were immediately enrolled in school. Young Victor was away at Hampton Institute and Marguerite remained at home for a very short period of time to help her mother care for her younger siblings. However, it wasn't long before she married local deli owner Mark Johnson and left the nest. From that union the first Daniel grandchild was born. She was named Elizabeth Ann, in memory of

Marguerite's sweet sister who died and who everyone fondly calls Betty Ann today. That beautiful gesture truly delighted my grandparents.

Unbeknownst to my grandmother, living just around the corner, was esteemed educator Dr. Mary McLeod Bethune, and these two phenomenal women would soon meet and find themselves traveling together to champion the cause for educating Black youth, and emancipating the great minds of their race.

As a staff reporter for *The Afro*, with her own column, there were simply no subjects too challenging or hellacious for my grandmother to address, and in just two short months she used her new found position to report on the injustices her family endured at CGI. She wrote a two-column article titled: "Trustees' Diverse Views Made Her Quit, Mrs. Daniel Says," after receiving a letter dated April 7th, from a resident of the Ridge, Maryland community.

The pain and grief endured by my grandparents after losing two children and dealing with the blatant racism against their eldest son at the hands of Catholic University, was simply the proverbial straw that broke the camel's back. During those dark days, with everything still being fresh in her mind, my grandmother fell silent. There were no words left to express the injustices that were levied against she and her family which left her completely heartbroken. She needed time to grieve, time to pray, and she needed to ask God why; and if she was to keep her wits about her, she needed time alone to think.

In an article dated June 30th, 1934, my grandmother addressed every issue detailed in the letter to her from the topics discussed in a private meeting held with the people of Ridge and a member of the Board of Trustees. The same straw that seemingly broke her spirit is the same straw that also instituted an awakening inside of her. She addressed eight topics in her article, including the one where she was accused of writing negative comments under the name of <u>C</u>ora <u>G</u>race <u>I</u>nman, pointing the lies in her direction. Under the subtitle, *Who is Cora Grace Inman?*, she wrote:

"I am in a position to say that Rev. John T. Gillard, Josephite of Archbishop Curley's archdiocese, used several AFRO columns last year to comment indignantly on matters appearing in "Of Interest to Catholics," an AFRO column published under the name "Cora Grace Inman," and guardedly pointed in my direction as the author of the column "biting the hands that feed her."

Later, some Catholics went to the AFRO office in person to request that the editor stop me from running the column. And I am in a position to say that although I have been thoroughly disgusted at the methods employed by officials at the church in sniping at me, this is the first occasion on which I have troubled myself to state that I never saw "Of Interest to Catholics" until after its appearance in the AFRO; that it was not my column at any time; and that I never contributed a line or a word to it."

Surprisingly enough, the initials of the so-called author of the article were C.G.I., however, I am confident to say that my grandmother wouldn't have had any problem writing such a column under her own name. She reported facts, not fiction!

With many personal and professional duties to carry out, she found little time to enjoy her younger children. Also, with my grandfather searching for educational employment opportunities, he often found himself being taken away from his home. With little help from their eldest daughter, now married with a child of her own, Grandma Constance often used the quiet of the night to think and write, once her remaining children went off to bed. She smoked cigarettes only when writing at night, but never in front of her children. She bounced many of her article ideas off of Sherman the family cat. All he could do was meow and that's all the feedback she needed. With my grandfather working in another state, the loyal feline served as her sounding board. Unfortunately, when the Daniel boys tried to show their baby brother Johnny how to shoot a gun, he accidently shot Sherman. The cat lived I was told, but he was never the same again.

Being unemployed my grandfather knew his family would endure certain hardships; however, my grandmother not only made ends meet, but she did what she had to do to care for their children. She made all of their clothes, stretched every meal, and mended every frayed piece of clothing to save money. If there was a hole in the sole of their shoes, the cereal boxes were used to reinforce them. My mother often said that the Shredded Wheat's box was her mother's choice of cereal boxes to fix their shoes, and she never allowed them to waste food. If they did not eat what she prepared for breakfast, they would surely see it again for lunch or maybe even dinner. Her favorite saying was "waste not, want not." Whether she realized it or not, my grandmother was truly a Proverbs 31 woman!

She is clothed with strength and dignity;
she can laugh at the days to come.
She speaks with wisdom,
and faithful instruction is on her tongue.
She watches over the affairs of her household
and does not eat the bread of idleness.
Her children arise and call her blessed;
her husband also, and he praises her:
"Many women do noble things,
but you surpass them all."

႙႙႙

Proverbs 31:25-29

CHAPTER 8

A DIVINE ENCOUNTER

Just living a few blocks from each other Constance and Dr. Bethune were destined to meet. I say it was divinely designed. They shared common interests and were determined to fight against the injustices of the American Negro through education, determination and enlightenment. She learned about my grandmother from her articles written in *The Afro-American* newspaper. Once these two iron-willed women met, they were truly inseparable and when she was on travel, they would write each other letters. They discussed everything from education, of course, to the comings and goings of my grandmother's children. No topic was off limit for these two women.

When Dr. Bethune was in town, my mother and her baby brother John would clean her home for a shiny new quarter to share between them. My mom often shared how she would apply wax on the banister and then slide down on it backwards to give it a beautiful shine. John on the other hand would stand at the base of it to make sure she didn't fall off or hurt herself.

Not only did these two phenomenal women share an intimate friendship with one another, they were connected professionally during my grandmother's tenure at the Farm Security Administration (FSA), a subagency of the Department of Agriculture formed in

1937. When her employment began at the agency in 1938, little did she know that she and Dr. Bethune would be working together once again in support of ensuring equitable practices for Black farmers. Although my grandparents had been gone from CGI for almost five years, Grandma Constance leveraged her position at the agency in a way to give back to Ridge, Maryland.

When FSA was in search of an impoverished rural community in which to establish a farm demonstration project, it was my grandmother who identified the town of Ridge as the community with the greatest need. Pictured in Andrea Hammer's book, *But Now When I Look Back*, most if not all of Roy Emerson Stryker's photographs of Southern Maryland illustrated the agricultural initiative that was spearheaded by my grandmother. My mom's Godmother Miss Annie is seen in one of the photos with a pressure cooker that also was a gift from FSA. When her daughter Veronica Reid interviewed my mother in 1989, she said, "… at that time… I'm gonna tell you the truth – the colored people got a lot of help from the Government, and the white people were jealous of it too, honey." Continuing she recalled how Grandma Constance sent a Home Demonstration Agent down to help the people and identified everybody who needed help. "One year, my mother received 150 chickens and the next year over 100 chickens and several hogs," Reid said. The residents of Ridge, Maryland didn't realize that my grandmother was the Guardian Angel behind FSA's benevolence. Little did they know that she never forgot them or their needs and continued to champion their causes. She simply saw it as an extension of the commitment she and my grandfather made when they moved to the area in 1924.

Impressed with her work at FSA, Dr. Bethune who was Founder of The National Council of Negro Women (NCNW), thought it would be equally beneficial to partner with her, so she solicited my grandmother's help. With its mission to lead and advocate for and empower women of African descent, their families and communities, Grandma Constance was most definitely on board. Dr. Bethune also led President Franklin D. Roosevelt's (FDR's) "Black Cabinet," an extraordinary advisory group made up of Black journalists, economists, attorneys, and sociologists. In the beginning she was the only woman represented, so she extended an invitation to my grandmother. Knowing that she was the second woman who was part of this secret organization made me admire her all the more.

Grandma Constance (center) attending an anti-lynching protest with members of the NAACP.

First Lady Eleanor Roosevelt and Dr. Bethune became friends and she hoped that many of her concerns that affected those who shared her race would reach the President. While FDR was keenly aware how much the "Black Cabinet" was to be credited for his success with winning the Black vote; in turn, just how beneficial was it going to be for those people of color who actually voted for him? As cited in Jill Watt's book, many Black and Brown voters asked, "Will the New Deal be a square deal for the Negro?" While the President may have addressed some of the concerns raised by his specialized advisory group, he also didn't want to lose his White southern voters. However, when the rubber met the road, and it came time for him to get behind the Federal anti-lynching legislation and desegregate the military, he most certainly dropped the ball.

On October 25th, 1940, Constance and Dr. Bethune had a meeting
with Mrs. Roosevelt at the White House to discuss jobs and
collective farming programs that would help lift Black people out of
poverty. Having the President's ear and a friendship with the First
Lady, Dr. Bethune and the Black
Cabinet had some wins, but was it
enough? It may not have been, but it
was a start. Behind the scenes this
elite group of Black intelligent minds
continued to work on behalf of their
people. However, they never received
the official recognition they deserved
from the President, but they certainly
changed history, leading from behind.

Pictured above: Grandma Constance
speaking out against FSA's practice
of using Federal dollars to pay the
poll taxes for White farmers, while
denying the same financial
assistance to Black farmers.

Pictured left: The press pass issued
to Grandma Constance for meeting
at the White House with she, Dr.
Bethune, and First Lade Eleanor
Roosevelt.

In 1942, Grandma Constance publicly complained about FSA's
practice of using Federal dollars to pay the poll taxes for White
farmers and denying the same assistance for Black farmers. Even
though she was totally correct in pointing out this injustice, she was
fired from her position after they offered her an additional $8,000 in
salary. I'm of the belief that it was hush money so she would turn a
blind eye to their discriminatory practices that she brought to their
attention. However, she responded with a resounding NO! Like
many other Blacks who were under the "so called" New Deal
programs, it cost my grandmother her job, but she had fought
tougher battles in earlier years and knew she could take on whatever

ailed her, armed with pen, paper and possibly the ear of the White House.

As mentioned previously, over a span of nine years, when not together, Grandma Constance and Dr. Bethune wrote to one another and their letters revealed so much about them, personally and professionally. She often and lovingly referenced my aunts and uncles in her correspondence. Uncle Bobby as well as my mom were always on Dr. Bethune's radar. One such letter dated November 24th, 1949, read as follows:

Mr. Robert A. Daniel
116 East Burlington Street
Iowa City, Iowa

My Dear Bobby –

Your card was so timely. I read it over several times to a group of people in my room. It was so thoughtful of you to send it. I hope that I may find the time to discover some recreation that will give me pleasure. It seems to me as if my whole life has been work and more work.

Constance and I are here trying to clear my desk. I know that you must feel very thankful in your heart, today, for the opportunity for study and for such broad contacts.

My blessings to you.

Sincerely yours,

Mary McLeod Bethune
Founder, President-Emeritus

During his time in school, and even after becoming an adult, she wrote letters of recommendation for him. Ultimately, he became an art professor and many of his original paintings adorn the homes of his children, nieces, and nephews to this day.

For years, my grandmother wrote for NCNW's house publication, *The Aframerican Women's Journal,* as well as edited columns, periodicals, and speeches for her dear friend. However, in January 1947, Dr. Bethune was greatly concerned about the affairs of her organization's Washington, D.C. office that were causing her much distress.

In a letter addressed to her friend who she affectionately called "Mother" Bethune out of endearment and respect, because she was 18 years her junior, she expressed her concern and shared what was on her mind. She mentioned how she had fully supported her because she wanted *The Journal* to be a "credit to the cause of all Negro women," whom she represented. Because of the discord that was being sown, she felt that as the editor, it put both she and the sponsors in an embarrassing position.

As a result, on February 6th, 1947, she submitted her letter of resignation and in part, she wrote: "… *with the publication of the winter issue of* The Journal *this week, I am withdrawing as editor."* She stated, *"My reason is the dismissal by your Executive Committee, without an opportunity for conference, of the four employees in your office who sought modicum of security through union recognition. The shocking disregard for human dignity with which these dismissals were accomplished was an affront to the sensibilities of the American community and effectively discount the committee's pleas of financial distress, as a basis for its action."*

Grandma Constance believed that the D.C. staff, who were supposed to help Dr. Bethune's cause, were hindering it by being reckless and were not on one accord with her vision and mission. She ended her letter, *"However, although I took over* The Journal *to support your leadership. As your editor I cannot put myself in conflict with your committee. As an informed citizen of good conscience, I cannot further serve your committee with its present policies. This leaves me no choice but to resign."*

Although my grandmother stepped down from her position, she remained loyal to her friend and the correspondence between them clearly showed that. She had major input in many of the columns that Dr. Bethune had written for the *Chicago Defender* in the early 1950's and even though she admitted that her health was declining in the letters written to my grandmother, both women pressed towards the mark to reach their ultimate goal of eradicating racial inequality.

However, sadly, on May 18th, 1955, Mary McLeod Bethune succumbed to her illness, which brought the NACW, NCNW, the Black Cabinet, Black America and Constance E. H. Daniel to a halt. In recognition of her lifetime activism, she was acknowledged "First Lady of Negro America," by *Ebony* magazine in 1949, as well as "The First Lady of The Struggle" because of her commitment to gain better lives for African Americans.

Grandma Constance was heartbroken hearing the news of her dear friend's death. They had worked so closely for years to ensure Black people would have better lives, in spite of the many racial barriers and obstacles that beset them. This marked the end of an era between these two remarkable women; however, my grandmother remained steadfast and unmovable when it came to continuing the mission and vision of her dear, dear friend.

CHAPTER 9

WELL DONE,
MY GOOD AND FAITHFUL SERVANT

After returning from Dr. Bethune's funeral my grandmother didn't allow all that she had gone through to distract her from her mission. So, she immersed herself into her writing and continued her syndicated column in *The Afro-American* titled, "Capital Close-Up" until 1957. She also wrote articles and short stories for the following publications – *Potomac Parade*, *Harper's Magazine*, *Ladies Home Journal*, *Cosmopolitan* and *Good Housekeeping*, to name a few. But she had her share of rejections as well.

An original sketch by Constance Daniel that accompanied her syndicated column in The Afro-American *titled* "Capital Close-up."

From time-to-time she traveled to New York City to see her doctor and her best friend from Tuskegee, Ruth Logan, but their visits were just too infrequent. However, during one of her trips, she met an author named Catherine Owens Peare who ironically was also friends with Dr. Bethune and who admired Constance's writing given how often she had spoken highly of my grandmother's talent. As a result, Ms. Peare wanted to see more of it. For those who aren't familiar with this acclaimed author, she wrote *The Helen Keller Story*, and many other infamous books, including one about Dr. Bethune. For obvious reasons, their connection was meant to be.

In a letter to Grandma Constance, Ms. Peare offered the following advice, in part, "…don't write the whole article. Write an outline of the idea and query around to see if a magazine is interested in that type of content." My grandmother probably thought to herself, easier said than done, and decided to submit her articles under an assumed name. It was hard enough getting work published as a woman, but as a Black woman made the process 10 times harder, however she didn't allow her race and gender deter her from submitting her writings. She was an intense writer and very passionate about who and what she wrote about. Not only did it bring her peace knowing that she could express herself through her articles and poems but writing also allowed her to escape from the many obstacles she faced and would continue to face.

When I first started reading her stories, her sense of humor admittingly was somewhat strange to me, but after re-reading them, and of course with a dictionary in hand, as if she were teaching me new words from Heaven, I began to hear her. I began to feel her. I began to embody her spirit, and just like that, I understood her. My grandmother wanted every man, woman, and child who had been repeatedly overlooked and undervalued to have a voice and to know that it mattered. From short stories to politics, she left no stone unturned.

She championed causes for the oppressed and continued to fight for civil rights and racial equality alongside her close friend and fellow educator Nannie Helen Burroughs, as well as furthered opportunities for women, beyond the simple duties of domestic housework. While serving as assistant principal at CGI, Grandma Constance advocated for a diverse curriculum that educated the students as opposed to just teaching them how to be domestic workers in the future. She exclaimed that their minds were far more superior than those who wanted to continue to oppress them. Her core beliefs are what connected she and Ms. Burroughs together in 1934. With iron sharpening iron, their friendship of more than 25 years stood the test of time, proving that my grandmother allowed those who were in the limelight to shine, while she successfully, and once again led from the rear.

In December 1959 she accepted a position as an Interviewer-Analyst with the Health and Welfare Council of the National Capital Area, working under its Director, Dr. Hylan Lewis. Mostly noted for spearheading a major child-rearing study during the Lyndon B. Johnson presidency, Dr. Lewis was part of the inner circle of scholars and Government officials who helped craft the President's Great Society policies.

She truly enjoyed her position with the Council, but unfortunately her contract ended in 1961. While searching for gainful employment, she continued to write short stories and articles for *Good Housekeeping*, *The Saturday Evening Post* and *Reader's Digest*, despite her declining health. My grandmother found little time to do the one thing rarely afforded her, and that was spending quality time with her children and grandchildren given that she often worked away from home helping to make ends meet. She rarely saw her sons Robert, who was teaching out of the area and John who was enlisted in the United States Navy. However her remaining children Victor Christopher, Dorothea, Marguerite, William, and Louise remained in the D.C. area. Thankfully, her daughter-in-law, Veronica (Victor's wife) was always a constant help to her and ensured that her home was well cared for while she was away.

However, having 12 grandchildren at the time and one on the way I wonder if she would have preferred to be elsewhere protesting about injustice or standing before a "firing squad" of Senators and Congressmen questioning her about equal rights for Black people.

Upon my grandfather's return home after a long separation from his family, he found his wife in poor health, but undeniably was elated to see her. Although they were used to being apart for months at a time, my grandmother, who rarely complained about her life, had failed to display her usual feistiness that granddad was accustomed to seeing on a regular basis. She was not the same woman who had faithfully served alongside him through the good and bad times from the day they were betrothed.

Sadly, on June 19th, 1962, at 3:45 p.m., Grandma Constance died at Providence Hospital in Washington, D.C., with her beloved Victor by her side. She was 68 years old, and her life was one well-lived, in spite of the numerous obstacles she had dealt with over the years. Not once did my grandmother ever waiver regarding her core beliefs and forged through life embodying the strength of her ancestors, and equipped with pen, paper and a superior mind. She had an innate ability to get her point across, with a vocabulary that would have made even Miriam Webster proud, and who used it methodically as her weapon of choice. If necessary, she meticulously expressed how she felt to any and everyone who crossed her path. After her death, there wasn't a day that my grandfather didn't have her in the forefront of his mind. However, a few years later, he joined her in the Heavenly realm, and they were together again, but this time in spirit.

As I conclude this story about my remarkable grandmother, I have no doubt that everyone who reads my book will understand why the title is what it is. Constance Eleanor Hazel Daniel was truly a force to be reckoned with and her legacy lives on within me, my siblings, and all of her living descendants who share her bloodline. Also, her name and work are still relevant today. In April 2021, my sisters Dana and Victoria were watching a televised documentary about Alpha Kappa Alpha Sorority and were shocked when they saw photographs of our grandmother as well as clippings of some of her newspaper articles that had been included in the footage. It goes without saying that her labor was not in vain, and I know she is smiling from the portals of Heaven with that stoic stance of hers as she continues to guide me, not from the rear, but from her heart.

Looking over her life and all that she accomplished, when she transitioned from her earthly assignment, I know God smiled at her and said, "Well done my good and faithful servant."

Victor and Constance Daniel on the porch of their home in the District of Columbia. Despite the insurmountable odds they faced, my grandmother never allowed them to crush their spirit, tenacity, or relentlessness. She was truly a force to be reckoned with!

~SELAH

A Loving Tribute to my late Grandmother, Constance Eleanor Hazel Daniel

Dear Grandmother Constance,

Because you paved the way many decades ago, I am a third generation published author and writer today. An unsung Shero, you were strong, brilliant, disruptive, a change agent, and a confident Black woman, long before it was popular, valued or appreciated! As a result, I stand on your shoulders.

Although I never had the opportunity to meet you, whenever I reflect on the greatness that you selflessly passed down to your children, grandchildren, and all who had the privilege to sit at your feet, I can't help but to think of excerpts from the powerful poem, "Our Deepest Fear" by Marianne Williamson.

In part it says, "Our deepest fear is not that we are inadequate. Our deepest fear is that we are powerful beyond measure. It is our light, not our darkness that most frightens us. And as we let our own light shine, we unconsciously give other people permission to do the same."

Thank you, Constance for being a light, a beacon of hope, an example of courage, and inspiration for so many, even still today. I am honored and grateful to call you Grandmother.

With love and admiration,
Your Granddaughter,

Victoria Lynn Boston

With Honor and Respect
To my late Great-Grandmother,
Constance Eleanor Hazel Daniel

Dearest Great-Grandmother Constance,

Your spirit is deep within the genetic fabric of our very being.

Your words of faith and determination, when nothing in your senses could illustrate why you should be so encouraged, have persevered through the generations that have followed your footsteps.

Your respect of planet and self has transcended through time, as we experience a homecoming of sorts: a remembering of all you have taught us about cultivation (of self, Earth, and our children).

Your unbreakable nature is something we all feel, every day when things get hard, and we aren't sure what gave us the strength to move forward.

We thank you. We honor you. We revere who you are. *Why? Because you didn't leave us empty handed. You provided the guide, a handbook if you will, of how to live fully in gratitude, with a life of service to all.*

How humbled we are to have your presence ever so near.

With love & light,
Your great-granddaughter,

Danielle

ABOUT THE AUTHOR

Donna M. Marshall is the granddaughter of Constance Eleanor Hazel Daniel. A native Washingtonian, she is a third-generation writer and a first-time author with the publishing of this book. She is currently retired from the healthcare management industry, where her career spanned over four decades, working in numerous medical specialty practices and hospitals. She also served as a volunteer medical liaison for her former church where she attended for 27 years. Marshall's mission is to help others navigate the healthcare system, which can be an intimidating and daunting task. "I'm here to make things easier for those who need it, just for the asking," she says. Her training with Cancer Treatment Centers of America, Our Journey of Hope, has afforded her many opportunities to assist men and women with various treatments for cancer.

A humble recipient of numerous Washington Hospital Center "BRAVO" awards for her excellence in delivering patient care, Marshall continues to assist patients, friends, and loved ones with their healthcare needs when requested. Her services and expertise have reached as far as Belarus, South Africa, South Korea, and Germany.

Not having any biological children of her own, Marshall takes great pride in assisting with the rearing of the grandchildren of South Africa's very own "Momma Africa," the renowned, late Miriam Makeba, as well as the children of Nelson and the late Bongi Lee. She also serves on the Executive Board of the Miriam Makeba Foundation.

She has spoken on numerous occasions during Black History Month at Washington, D.C.-area schools; walking proudly in her late mother's footsteps.

As one of seven children, Marshall is very close with her family and delights in their accomplishments. She currently lives in Florida with her husband of 30 years and enjoys swimming, bicycle riding, and the simplicities of life.